What experts are saying about

When There's No Mechanic

by Jim Gaston

" Full of practical information on safe driving, maintenance, and car repair. Written in non-technical language, this unique book is highly recommended for libraries."

- Library Journal

" Helpful safety, maintenance, and repair tips in a basic car and driving guide."

- Booklist Magazine

" For most of us, car repair is intimidating. When There's No Mechanic goes a long way to reducing the anxiety of car repairs and may even encourage you to do-it-yourself."

- Jack Gillis
author of The Car Book

" Covers virtually any problem you may encounter with a car."

- Dan Miller
American Driver Education

What experts are saying about

When There's No Mechanic

by Jim Gaston

" Helpful information and trouble shooting tips."
- <u>The Bookwatch</u>

". . . everyday language and well documented."
- George Hensel, editor
<u>Driving School Association of America</u>

" This books describes how to keep your car running, what service it needs, or does not need. Keep a copy in the glove compartment."
- <u>News Press</u>
St Joseph, MO

" <u>When There's No Mechanic</u> contains specific information in well organized chapters. It is a very helpful and easy to follow guide."
- <u>Patrician Productions, NY</u>

" As host of the weekly radio program **CAR KEYS**, Jim Gaston's help with peoples automotive problems is much appreciated."
- Jim Sackett
<u>WDNC Radio</u>

Revised Edition

When There's No Mechanic

127 Important Things to Know About Your Car

Jim Gaston

CoNation Publications
SAN 297-4029
703-W Ninth Street
Durham NC 27705
USA

Second Edition Completely Revised

Printed in the United States of America

Cover by Kachergis Book Design

P-Catalog In Publication Data:
       Gaston, Jim
       When There's No Mechanic
       127 Important Things To Know About Your Car
       Includes Index. 272 p. 21 cm.
       ISBN 1-879699-23-0 (Softcover)
       1. Automobile: Maintenance & Repair.
       2. Automobile Driving 3. Consumer Education.
       I. Title. TL152.G   1994   629.28
       LC Catalog Card Number: 91-71419

**Also by
Jim Gaston**

The Green Machine

The Car Care Logbook

Talking About Cars

Trouble Shooting Tips

Car Care

**CoNation Publications
703-W Ninth Street
Durham NC 27705**

About The Author

Jim Gaston earned a mechanical engineering degree from North Carolina State University and graduated from the North Carolina Division of Motor Vehicles Instructor Development Course. He teaches at Durham Technical Community College and is a regular guest on the radio program **CAR KEYS**.

> " My goal is to help you have a long and happy relationship with your car. I hope you enjoy this book and keep your car running safely for many years. Drive carefully. "
>
> **- Jim Gaston**

If you have a question about your car, write to Mr. Gaston at the CoNation address or via CompuServe #71732.471.

Mr. Gaston has produced other books, audio tapes and computer programs on car care. The books are available from your local bookstore or directly from CoNation Publications. An order form is included at the back of this book.

If you would like FREE information about any of these items, send your name and address to CoNation today.

Table Of Contents

Chapter 10 Steering & Suspension (cont.)

Chapter 11 Safety Items 163

Chapter 12 Good Driving Habits 177

Chapter 13 Off-Road Driving 185

Chapter 14 Maintenance 203

Chapter 14 Maintenance (cont.)

Chapter 15 Troubleshooting 221

Chapter 16 Accidents 245

Glossary 255

Index 267

⚠ WARNING - DISCLAIMER

This book is based on generally accepted procedures for operating, maintaining and repairing a car. These procedures may differ depending on the particular car or situation involved. The reader must use caution and consult the owners manual, shop manual, or a trained technician whenever necessary. Improper operation, maintenance, or repairs may cause serious injuries or car damage.

The information contained in this book is accurate and complete to the best of our knowledge. However, the publisher and author specifically disclaim any and all liability for accident, injury, or other loss and risk incurred as a direct or indirect consequence of the recommendations, advice, or information presented in this book.

Consult the owners manual, shop manual, or a trained technician for specific maintenance and repair recommendations about your car.

Safety Is No Accident !

Second Edition Preface

It is a wonderful time to own and drive a car. You can cruise down the highway in comfort at speeds your grandparents could not imagine. You depend on your car to get you where you want to go and the last thing you need is a breakdown or major repair. This book can help you keep your car running great for many years.

Automotive changes

The automotive industry is constantly changing and cars are getting more complex each year with additional computers and safety devices. However, if you want to keep your car running safely for a long time, easy preventive maintenance and safe driving habits are your best bets. You might not want to do the actual repairs yourself, however, just knowing more about your car, how it operates, what service it needs (or doesn't need) can save you time and hassles down the road.

Good Car Care

Every car needs good care if you expect them to be reliable and economical. Fortunately, the easy preventive maintenance is much less expensive and safer than allowing the car to breakdown. If you find cars intimidating, this book can help explain the mysteries of how the car works, and important things you can do to keep it running great for years and years.

Good Communication

Learn more about your car so you will be able to communicate effectively with the mechanic. You do not have to become a mechanic to understand your car.

" For most of us, car repair is intimidating. <u>When There's No Mechanic</u> goes a long way to reducing the anxiety of car repairs and may even encourage you to do-it-yourself."
- Jack Gillis
author of <u>The Car Book</u>

Non-Technical Language

This book is written in easy to understand language. The technical terms are explained in non-technical ways and a complete expanded glossary can be found at the back of the book.

". . . everyday language and well documented."
- George Hensel, editor
<u>Driving School Association of America</u>

Proven Textbook

The first edition of this book has been used as the textbook in many basic car care classes and has helped other people learn how to keep their cars running great. This revised edition has been updated and expanded to include even more helpful information.

Introduction

Driving a car is one of the most dangerous things you do each day. Car accidents are a leading cause of deaths and injuries each year; especially among younger people. Despite recent advances in car safety and tougher traffic laws, driving remains a hazardous activity.

Buying a car is also a major financial decision; the second most expensive item you will probably buy. Transportation cost may total up to 15% of your annual expenses while the car depreciates and repair cost skyrockets. Despite new demands for improved public transportation, you depend on your car to get you where your want to go.

What should you do?

First, you do **not** have to become a mechanic to drive a car or do easy maintenance. The best way to save time and money on car repair is to have a basic understanding of how the car operates and what service it needs (or doesn't need).

Unfortunately, the owners manual does not always provide enough information and the shop manual is too technical. This book, however, can be your personal guide to driving and maintenance and help you gain control over the perils of owning and operating a car.

Drive Safely

How can you avoid a serious accident or roadside breakdown and maintain the car so it will run for at least 12 years or 200,000 miles? You can achieve these important goals with a good car, good driving habits, and regular preventive maintenance. These three factors are equally important in keeping the car in reliable condition.

This book does not describe how to do major car repairs and is not intended as a substitute for the owners manual or shop manual. It does provide basic information about driving a car and easy steps you can take to help prevent many common car problems.

Informed Consumer

This book will also help you to become an informed automotive consumer. Learning more about your car will help you to understand which products or services your car really needs, and which ones are a waste of money. Sometimes it is necessary to spend a little more money to get a much better value, other times doing nothing at all is the wise choice.

Learn more about your car and drive with confidence. This book will help you become a safer driver and smarter automotive consumer.

DRIVING EMERGENCIES

Car accidents can be avoided when both the speed and direction of the car are kept within safe limits. In other words, slow down and watch where you are going. Study this chapter carefully and learn what to do in case of a driving emergency. Additional safe driving tips can be found in Chapters 12 and 13. Always drive defensively and watch for changing road conditions.

Safety is no accident. Learn about safety before learning about an accident.

Stop The Car

Do not press the brake pedal too hard when stopping your car. Slamming-on-the-brakes can cause the wheels to stop turning, or lock-up, which will make the car slide. If the wheels are not turning, you cannot steer the car and it will take longer to stop. The tires will also be damaged from sliding on the road. Stop the car quickly by applying the brakes firmly without locking-up the wheels. Newer cars may have Anti-lock Brake Systems (ABS) designed to prevent skids, and allow you to steer while braking hard.

> Avoid sudden stops by driving below the speed limit and according to the road conditions. Allow adequate stopping distance in front of your car. Do not tailgate other cars.

Turn The Car

When turning the car, move the steering wheel slowly. Turning the steering wheel quickly can cause the car to go out-of-control and even turn over. The faster the car is moving, the slower you should turn the steering wheel. Avoid sudden turns when driving fast.

Never turn the steering wheel when the car is sitting still. This is called dry-steering and will damage the tires and steering system.

A Flat Tire

A tire can go flat suddenly or "blow out" when the car is driven over a sharp object. A blowout can also occur when the tire is overinflated, very old, or worn out. A tire can go flat slowly if it is not attached to the rim correctly or if it is leaking.

When A Tire Goes Flat

The tire may go flat quickly and start making flapping noises as the car pulls to one side. If the tire looses air slowly, the car will slowly start pulling to one side as the tire begins to make flapping noises. The car will pull towards the side with the flat tire.

1. Take your foot off of the fuel pedal and hold the steering wheel with both hands. Control the direction of the car, but avoid sudden turns.

Do not brake quickly, which might cause the car to spin out of control.

2. Apply the brakes gently or just allow the car to slowly coast to a stop in a safe level place on

3

the side of the road. Move the car off of the road and out of the way of other cars. Driving the car with a flat tire can damage the tire, wheel, and steering system.

3. Refer to Chapter 15 - Changing A Flat Tire

Driving On Uneven Roads

A hard surface road has a shoulder or low edge near the outside. When roads are being repaired, some sections of the road may be uneven. Dirt roads can develop deep grooves, or ruts, after a heavy rain.

Deep grooves in the road can cause the steering wheel to spin quickly and the car may suddenly change direction. This can damage your fingers and the steering system.

When The Car Runs Off The Road

When a tire drops onto a lower road surface, the car will suddenly pull towards the lower side. Do not turn or brake quickly, which might cause the car to spin out-of-control or turn over.

1. Take your foot off the fuel pedal and hold the steering wheel with both hands. Control the direction of the car, avoid sudden turns.

2. Apply the brakes gently or just allow the car to slow down gradually, while keeping the other wheels of the car on the higher road surface.

3. When the car has slowed to about 10 MPH, check the traffic and road conditions. Then steer the car back onto the level road.

4. Test the steering wheel and brakes before resuming high speed driving.

Avoid Uneven Roads

1. Watch the road conditions carefully, especially while driving fast and in bad weather.

2. Stay in your lane, away from the shoulder of the road.

3. Drive slow on uneven roads.

Brake Failure

The brakes will not work properly when the brake fluid level is low or the brake pads are worn or wet. Test the brakes after driving through deep water. Press the brake pedal gently while the car is moving to dry the brake pads.

When The Brakes Do Not Work

1. Quickly pump the brake pedal several times. This will normally stop the car.

2. Apply the parking brake, or hand brake, firmly. Do not allow the tires to lock-up or skid.

Do not drive a car when the brakes are not working properly. Have all brake repairs done according to the shop manual.

Avoid Brake Problems

Check the brake fluid level and maintain a FULL level each WEEK. Inspect the brakes pads and brake lines every 6 MONTHS. Repair the brakes, according to the shop manual, as needed.

After any brake repair or inspection, test drive the car at slow speeds in a safe place before driving on the highway. Listen carefully for any unusual noise.

Skidding

A car can skid, or slide sideways, whenever you turn or stop very quickly (especially on slippery roads). Normally, the back end of the car will slide to one side. Use extra caution to avoid a skid when pulling a trailer. Drive slower and allow additional stopping distance.

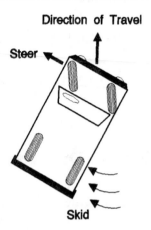

Direction of Travel

Steer

Skid

When The Car Skids

1. Release all the pedals: Fuel, Brake, and Clutch.

> Using the brakes while the car is skidding will make the car skid more.

2. Turn the steering wheel in the direction you want the <u>front</u> of the car to go. If the back of the car is skidding to the left, turn the steering wheel to the left, or Counter ClockWise (CCW).

3. Allow the car to slow down until you regain control.

Avoid Skids

Apply the brakes gently. Avoid sudden stops. Slow down before turning. Drive slower on slippery roads. Bridges and shady spots in the road may be very slick in cold weather.

Engine Overheats

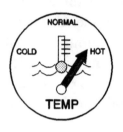

The engine will overheat when there is a problem with the cooling system, such as a low radiator fluid level, or a broken radiator hose, or a defective thermostat. Driving fast, low engine oil, improper engine timing, or using the A/C can also cause the engine to overheat.

Do not open the hood or remove the radiator cap which may allow very hot steam from the radiator to burn you.

When The Engine Overheats

Overheating can cause steam from the engine, the temperature light will come ON, or the gauge will point to HOT.

1. Turn the heater to HOT and the fan on HIGH. Turn the A/C OFF. The heater removes heat from the engine.

2. Stop the car in a safe place. Allow the engine to idle for one minute.

3. If, after one minute, the engine is still very HOT, turn the key switch to OFF.

4. Allow the engine to cool slowly for at least one hour before attempting any repairs.

Check the level of radiator fluid each WEEK. Maintain a full level of fluid, but do not overfill. Replace the radiator fluid using a 50-50 mixture of water and coolant (anti-freeze) every 2 YEARS. Replace the radiator hoses, radiator cap, belts, thermostat, and water pump every 4 YEARS.

Locate and repair any leak in the cooling system to avoid engine damage.

Low Oil Pressure

Low oil pressure can be caused by a low level of engine oil, dirty oil filter, or the wrong type (viscosity) of oil.

If the engine looses oil pressure, it will make clicking sounds, or the warning light will come ON, or the gauge will be very LOW. Low oil pressure can cause major engine damage.

When The Oil Pressure Is Low

1. Stop the car in a safe place and turn the engine OFF.

2. Use the dipstick to check the oil level.

3. Look for oil leaks near the engine. Check the oil filter and oil drain plug.

4. Add more oil through the oil fill cap until the dipstick shows a FULL level.

Do not drive the car when the **oil pressure** or **oil level** is very LOW.

 Check the engine oil level with the dipstick each WEEK. Add more oil, as needed, to maintain a FULL level. Change the oil and filter every 2 MONTHS.

Windows Fogs

Fog on the windows is actually small drops of water from the air which appear when certain humidity and temperature conditions exist. In cold weather, the fog can form ice. When the windows have fog, you cannot see where you are going. The fog can be either on the inside or the outside of the windows.

When The Windows Fogs

Do not drive the car when the windshield or windows have fog or your visibility is limited.

1. If the fog is on the outside, use the wipers to remove it. If the fog is on the inside, wipe it off with your hand or a cloth.

2. Turn the heater ON (HOT) and direct the hot air onto the window. Use the A/C to remove moisture from the air. Some newer cars automatically run the A/C with the heater for this purpose.

Some cars have an electric heater on the rear window operated by a switch on the dashboard. This heater uses electrical power from the battery to heat very small wires attached to the glass.

Car Fire

A car fire is usually caused by a fuel leak or an electrical short circuit.

When The Car Is On Fire

1. Stop the car.
2. Turn the key switch to OFF.
3. Get everyone out of and away from the car.
4. Send for help.

Do not open the hood, which may allow the fire to spread. Heat near the fuel tank or battery can cause an explosion.

Do not put water on an electrical fire or burning fuel. This can cause the fire to spread faster. A Carbon-Dioxide (CO_2), Halon, or A-B-C fire extinguisher will smother the fire, if used properly.

Avoid A Fire

Use the proper size fuses (AMP capacity). Install and repair electrical items properly according to the shop manual. Fix all leaks in the fuel system immediately. Keep sparks or open flames away from the car.

Fuel Pedal Gets Stuck

If the fuel pedal gets stuck, the speed of the car engine may increase or the car may continue moving, even when the pedal is released and the brakes are applied.

When The Fuel Pedal Gets Stuck

1. Shift the transmission lever to (N) Neutral. The engine may start turning very fast.

> Do not turn the key switch when the car is moving. The steering wheel and brakes could malfunction. Wait until the car stops before turning the key switch to **OFF**.

2. Stop the car on the side of the road, using the brakes gently.

3. When the car stops, turn the key switch OFF.

Avoid A Stuck Fuel Pedal

Check the fuel pedal before starting the engine. Keep carpets or floormats away from the pedals. Check the fuel pedal linkage every 6 MONTHS. If the rubber pad on the pedal wears out, replace it.

13

Engine Stops

Whenever the engine suddenly stops, the problem is probably the ignition system or fuel system (out of gas). A gasoline engine may stop if it gets wet.

When The Engine Stops

1. Shift the transmission lever to Neutral (N).

2. Stop the car on the side of the road, using the brakes gently. If the car has power brakes or power steering, extra force may be needed to stop or steer when the engine is not running.

Avoid Engine Problems

Do not run out of gas. Stop to fill-up when the fuel level is about 1/4 Tank (before Empty). Running out of fuel can damage some engines. Slow down when crossing wet areas to avoid getting the engine wet. Water can cause a gasoline engine to stop suddenly.

Tune-up the engine each YEAR. Refer to Chapter 6 for more information about the tune-up. All cars need a tune-up and regular maintenance for reliable service.

Impatient Driver

People in a hurry can become very impatient. Impatience, however, is more likely to cause you to have an accident than it is to help you be on time. Ironically, many traffic jams and road side breakdowns are caused by people who have neither the time nor the money to waste.

Impatient drivers tend to overlook basic safe driving practices and because they are in such a hurry to arrive, they forget to enjoy the trip.

Avoid Impatience

1. Slow down. Being late is not as bad as having an accident or getting a speeding ticket.

2. Plan ahead and allow adequate travel time.

Do not be in a hurry to have an accident or get a speeding ticket.

Avoid heavily traveled areas and times of day. Going to work at 8 o'clock may mean more traffic than traveling the same route at 7:30 or 8:30. Work out a better schedule with your employer to save yourself from rush hour traffic.

Drowsy Driver

Driving, especially long trips, can be extremely boring. The sound of the engine and movement of the car can cause drowsiness. Stay alert when you are driving.

When You Become Drowsy

Your reflexes are slower and you may overlook warning signs from the car, such as excessive speed or strange noises. Some people even fallen asleep while driving.

> Exhaust gases from the engine contain carbon monoxide: a colorless, odorless, tasteless, but extremely fatal gas.

1. Roll down the window to get some fresh air.
2. Cool down by adjusting the A/C or heater.
3. Stop the car. Exercise or drink some coffee.
4. If you are still drowsy, let someone else drive.

> Do not operate the engine in an enclosed space, such as the garage, without good ventilation. Do not stay inside a stationary car while the engine is running if the windows are closed.

Avoid Drowsiness

Keep your eyes moving while driving. This is called scanning. Watch where the car is going, but also glance to the sides, behind the car, and at the gauges often. Do not daydream while driving or stare in one direction for a long time. On long trips, stop every hour to stretch. Do not drive more than six hours each day.

DO NOT DRINK AND DRIVE.

Do not drive after drinking any alcoholic beverage or taking any medication which might cause drowsiness.

Alcohol is involved in almost one-half of all fatal car accidents. Do not let someone drive if you know they have been drinking.

Distracted Driver

Distractions can happen very quickly and unexpectedly. Watch where you are going and think about what you are doing. Whenever the car is moving and your attention is diverted from controlling the speed or direction of the car, even for a moment, there is the possibility of a serious accident.

Do not be distracted from controlling the speed and direction of the car while it is moving. Keep your mind on driving the car.

Avoid Distractions

1. Avoid eating, drinking, or smoking while driving.

2. If an insect gets into the car, stop the car before attempting to catch it.

3. Do not be distracted by passengers in the car who are talking, throwing things, or playing music. Fasten children securely in their car seats and lock the doors before starting a trip.

PARTS & TOOLS

Every car needs some spare parts and tools. If you drive in remote areas or on a long trip, you may need additional items. Check the tool kit in your car and add additional items, if necessary. Purchase spare parts from a local auto store, whenever possible, so you will not have to keep a large inventory in your garage. However, if the local supply is not reliable, stock up on the needed parts and tools, so you will have them when you need them.

Some tools require special training. Using the wrong tool can cause injuries or car damage.

Car Parts

All replacement parts are not the same quality. The higher priced parts are usually better quality and should last longer. The cheapest parts may look like the expensive part, but they may not last very long and can cause serious car damage. Beware of poor quality look-alike parts which can cause damage to the car. These parts will not have any name or address on the box and may be very cheap.

Rebuilt and Remanufactured Parts

Rebuilt usually means a part that has been repaired and is in working condition. A rebuilt part should have some type of warranty or guarantee in addition to being much less expensive than a new or remanufactured part.

Remanufactured usually means a part that has been completely disassembled, tested, and put together in like-new condition. A remanufactured part should have a warranty or guarantee just like the new part; however, it should be less expensive than the new part.

The cheapest parts can be found in the junk yard on similar type cars. These parts rarely have any warranty or guarantee.

The Best Parts

The original manufacturers replacement parts are usually the best quality; however, they will also be the most expensive, too. These parts may be available at discount stores or you can often save money by shopping for quality name brand parts on sale.

The Life Of A Car Part

Most car parts have an estimated life expressed in either in time (months or years) or distance (miles). If the life is given in miles, divide by 2000 to estimate the number of months. This is only a rule-of-thumb; they may last a longer or shorter time/distance depending on how you drive the car and the local driving conditions.

The Guarantee

Most car parts come with some type of guarantee or warranty. A registration card or other written records may be needed or a trained technician may have to install the part.

> Do not wait until a problem arises to read the guarantee, because it may be too late. Read the guarantee when buying the part.

Information About The Car

The following information should be available for your car. Learn how to safely drive and maintain your car to keep it in good operating condition for many years.

1. **The Owners Manual.** The owners manual contains specific information about operating and maintaining the car.

2. **When There's No Mechanic.** This book contains useful information and tips about your car.

> Keep a copy of **When There's No Mechanic** in the car for easy reference.

3. **The Shop Manual.** The shop manual contains specific information about repairing the car. Shop manuals are available from the car dealer, library, or bookstore.

4. **A Log Book.** The log book is used to record the maintenance and repair work, fuel economy, and trip records. Show the log book to the mechanic when normal service or repairs are done.

Keep A Log Book

A log book can help you remember to do necessary preventive maintenance. It should also increase the value of your car by providing written proof of proper service.

1. **Record any maintenance or repair.** Each time your car is serviced or repaired, write down the date, odometer (milage), work done, invoice number, and the cost of the job. List the labor and parts cost separately, if possible.

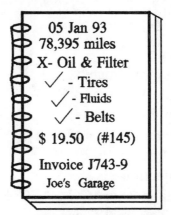

```
05 Jan 93
78,395 miles
X- Oil & Filter
  ✓ - Tires
  ✓ - Fluids
  ✓ - Belts
$ 19.50   (#145)

Invoice J743-9
Joe's Garage
```

2. **Record the fuel mileage.** Each time you fill up, write down the date, mileage (odometer), and gallons of fuel purchased.

A log book is available from CoNation for only $4.95. Use the ORDER FORM at the back of this book to order your copy today.

23

3. **Record other trip information.** Record the
   number of business miles driven each day. Cars
   with a trip odometer can be used to easily
   measure distances of daily trips.

Items For All Cars

Tool Kit

1. Owners Manual
2. Flashlight
3. Spare Tire
4. Jack
5. Lug Wrench
6. Tire Pressure Gauge
7. Adjustable Wrench
8. Vise-grip Pliers
9. Screwdrivers (Flat and Star)
10. Jumper-Cables
11. Eye Protection
12. Fire Extinguisher (CO_2, ABC, Halon)
13. Battery Terminal Cleaner
14. Knife
15. Fuses (assorted AMP sizes)
16. Radiator Sealer
17. Hose Clamps
18. Electrical or Duct Tape
19. Rubber Hose (1/4 ID X 6 feet)
20. Matches or Lighter
21. Small File
22. Wire or Coat Hanger

First Aid Kit

1. Band-aids (assorted sizes)
2. Aspirin
3. Soap
4. Insect Repellent
5. Scissors
6. Needle and Thread
7. Razor Blades
8. Safety Pins
9. Salt Tablets
10. Moleskin Adhesive
11. Tape
12. Thermometer
13. Snakebite Kit
14. Sterile Gauze Pads
15. Antacid Tablets
16. Antiseptic Cream
17. Antihistamines
18. Elastic Bandages
19. Matches (waterproof)
20. Baking Soda (neutralizes battery acid)
21. Special Medication

Put a First Aid Manual in the kit. Write down important telephone numbers, such as your doctor, the poison control center, and your nearest relative.

Items For A Long Trip

1. Food and Water
2. Wrenches (Metric or Standard)
3. Hacksaw Blade
4. Air Pump
5. Gloves
6. Sandpaper
7. Rope or Tow Chain
8. Misc. - Nuts, Bolts, Nails, Washers, and Screws.
9. Shop Manual

Do not carry fuel inside your car. Use a special container for fuel.

Spare Parts

Every Year

1. Oil Filters (6)
2. Lubricants / Fluids (as needed)
3. Fuel Filter(s)
4. Air Filter
5. Sparkplugs (1 per cylinder)
6. PCV Valve and Filter (Gasoline Engine)
7. Distributor Cap and Rotor (Gasoline Engine)
8. Carburetor Cleaner (Engine with Carburetor)

Every 2 Years
1. Windshield Wipers (Inserts)

Every 4 Years

1. Tires
2. Wheels Bearings (4 sets)
3. Universal Joints (C.V. Joints)
4. Shock Absorbers (Struts)
5. Ball Joints
6. Brake Pads (4 sets)
7. Flexible Brake Hoses (4)
8. Fuel Pump
9. Fuel Cap
10. Muffler (Catalytic Converter)
11. Battery and Cables
12. Engine Belt(s) and Timing Belt
13. Thermostat and Water Pump
14. Radiator Hoses and Clamps
15. Radiator Cap
16. Clutch Release Bearing (Manual Trans.)
17. Clutch Plate and Cover (Manual Trans.)
18. Injectors (Fuel Injection Engines)
19. Carburetor Kit (Engine with Carburetor)
20. Sparkplug Wires

Miscellaneous Spare Parts

1. Tire Valves and Caps
2. Cables (Speedometer-Tachometer-Fuel-Clutch)
3. Head Gasket
4. Oil Seals
5. Headlights and Taillights
6. Rubber Bushings

Maintenance Tools

Typical Tools Needed For Car Maintenance

1. Shop Manual
2. Socket Set (Standard or Metric)
3. Reversible Rachet Drive (for sockets)
4. Rachet Extensions and Universal Joints
5. Assorted Screwdrivers (Flat and Star/Phillips)
6. Hammer
7. Chisels
8. Long-Nose Pliers
9. Circuit Tester or VOM (Volt-Ohm Meter)
10. Jack Stands (2)
11. Vacuum Gauge / Fuel Pump Tester
12. Compression Gauge
13. Wire Brush
14. Grease Gun with a flexible extension
15. Feeler Gauge / Gap Tool
16. Hub Puller
17. Torque Wrench

A torque wrench is needed to tighten parts to a specified tightness. If the parts are too loose, they may come apart. If they are too tight, they may be damaged. The shop manual should indicate exactly how tight each part should be.

40 lbs. Force

1 ft.

1 ft. X 40 lbs. = 40 ft-lbs.
Distance X Force = Torque
Metric Units = NM

ELECTRICAL SYSTEMS

The key switch allows electrical power stored in the battery to operate the starter and turn parts inside the engine. After the engine starts running, the alternator produces the electricity needed to operate the car and recharge the battery.

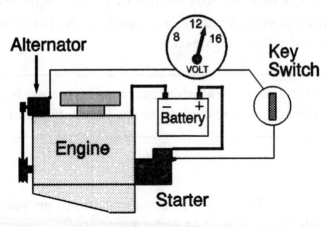

Key Switch

The key switch, or the
ignition switch, has four
functions: Off/Lock, Acc, On,
and Start. It is usually located
on the right side of the
steering column; however, it
can be installed on the
dashboard or on the left side
of the steering column.

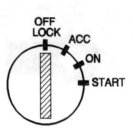

1. **OFF/LOCK.** The key can be inserted or
   removed only from the LOCK position. The
   steering wheel cannot turn and no electricity is
   available to the accessories or ignition.

 Do not turn the key switch to LOCK while the
car is moving. The steering wheel cannot turn and
the car cannot be steered.

Some cars have a safety button which must be
pressed to move the key to the **LOCK** position.

---

2. **ACC.** The ACCessories position provides
   electrical power to some items (radio, wipers,
   clock), but not the ignition system.

3. **ON.** When the key is in the ON position, electricity is available to all the accessories and the ignition system. The battery can loose power if the key is in the ON position when the engine is OFF.

The headlights are controlled by a light switch, not the key switch. The light switch should be **OFF** whenever the engine is not running. Otherwise, the battery will lose power very quickly and may not start the engine.

---

4. **START.** The START position allows electrical power stored in the battery to operate the starter. The switch should return to the ON position automatically when the key is released.

Safety starting switches are sometimes installed to monitor the position of the transmission shifting lever, clutch pedal, brake pedal, or seat belts. Refer to Chapter 11 for more information about the safety starting switches.

Key Switch Maintenance

Do not hold the key switch in the START position for more than 10 seconds. If the engine does not start, wait several minutes to allow the starter to cool off, before trying again. Do not turn the key switch to the START position when the engine is running.

Repairing The Key Switch

1. When the switch is stuck in the LOCK position, turn the steering wheel slightly to the right or left (relieve pressure on the locking mechanism) while turning the key gently.

2. Use a little dry switch lubricant, such as graphite, if necessary. Do not get water, dirt, or oil in the switch.

Electrical System Indicators

Warning Light

The warning light indicates when the battery is being charged. When the light is OFF, the alternator is producing electricity needed to operate the car and charge the battery. When the light is ON, the battery is loosing power.

Testing The Warning Light

1. The battery warning light should come ON when the key is turned to the ON position (before engine starts).

2. The warning light should go OFF after the engine starts.

Ammeter

The ammeter indicates when the battery is being charged. POSitive (+) charge means that the alternator is producing electricity needed to operate the car and recharge the battery. NEGative (-) charge means that the battery is loosing power.

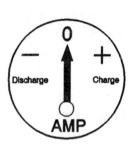

Testing The Ammeter

1. The ammeter should indicate a NEGative (-) charge while the key is in the START position.

2. The ammeter should indicate a POSitive (+) charge while the engine is running.

Voltmeter

Low voltage means the battery is loosing power. High voltage means the battery is overcharged or the voltage regulator is damaged.

Testing The Voltmeter

The voltmeter should indicate between 12 and 14 volts (12 volt system) while the engine is running.

Repairing The Electrical System Indicators

1. Check the fuse box for a broken fuse.
2. Clean and tighten the connections on the electrical indicators.

Battery

The battery stores electrical power needed primarily to start the engine. When the key switch is turned to the START position, electrical power from the battery goes to the starter. After the engine starts, the alternator produces the electricity needed to operate the car and recharge the battery.

The battery is a large plastic box which contains metal plates submerged in a mixture of water and acid (battery fluid). There are two large wires, or cables, connected to the battery. The positive cable is connected to the starter and the electrical accessories. The negative cable (ground) is connected directly to the metal car frame.

Negative ground (used in most cars) means that the negative battery cable is connected to the car frame. A **positive ground** system would have the positive battery cable connected to the car frame.

A 12-Volt electrical system is standard in most cars; however, there are 6 and 24 Volt systems. Always check the electrical system carefully before installing electrical equipment or jump-starting the car.

When the battery is charged, some of the water in the battery fluid evaporates. A battery that is allowed to run dry (when the fluid does not cover the metal plates) may not be able to start the car and can be permanently damaged. If the battery has removable caps, check the fluid level each week.

Add only pure distilled water to the battery.

Volts

The battery is divided into several sections; each section produces about two volts, therefore, a 12 volt battery will have six sections. Almost all car batteries are 12 volt, however, the power (amps) of the battery can vary greatly.

Amps

The size of the battery normally determines the amperage, or available power. A bigger battery should have more amps and more power. Cold Cranking Amps (CCA) is the amount of power available when the battery is cold.

Cold Weather

Cold weather is hard on the battery because:
1. A cold battery has less power available.
2. A cold engine is harder to turn.
3. Cold fuel does not burn easily.

Check the condition of the battery before cold weather arrives. A battery that starts the car easily in the summertime may be unable to start the car in cold weather.

A very cold battery can freeze. Keep the battery fully charged to prevent it from freezing. If you add water to the battery in cold weather, drive the car for about 10 minutes to mix the water and acid.

Battery Maintenance

1. Check the battery each week. It should be secure. Do not overtighten the bracket holding the battery. This can damage the battery.

2. Check the level of battery fluid. Add distilled water, if necessary. A Maintenance Free battery may be sealed and should not need water.

3. Every 6 Months clean the battery, if necessary. Grease and dirt on the outside of the battery can cause it to lose power.

4. Clean or tighten the battery cables, if necessary. Anti-corrosion battery terminal washers are inexpensive, easy to install, and can prevent corrosion near the terminals.

Testing The Battery

1. The starter motor should turn easily when key switch is in the START position.

2. The battery should be almost full of fluid (water and acid) and not have any leaks.

Repairing The Battery

If the battery loses power and cannot start the engine, jump-start the engine or recharge the battery. Refer to Chapter 15 for information.

> Wear eye protection when working near a battery. The battery fluid contains sulfuric acid which is very corrosive. If the battery acid is spilled, wash the spill with plenty of water and use baking soda to neutralize the acid.

1. A slow charge (trickle charge) is the best way to recharge a dead battery. A quick charge in less than one hour can overheat the battery and cause damage. Do not have sparks or heat near a battery. The battery produces dangerous gases and could explode.

2. Disconnect the battery when making repairs to any electrical part of the car or when welding parts on the car.

> Do not disconnect the battery while the engine is running. This can damage the alternator or electrical system.

3. If the battery is damaged or cannot be charged, replace it. Most car batteries should last about four years. Do not add chemicals to the battery fluid.

4. Buy a bigger replacement battery. A battery with more CCA will provide more power for starting the car in cold weather and should last longer.

Starter

When the key is turned to the START position, the starter turns parts inside the engine in order to get the fuel-air mixture burning. The starter is 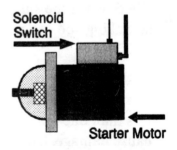 a small electric motor which uses power from the battery. It is located near the bottom of the engine.

There are two large cables on the battery. One cable is attached to the car frame. The other cable, usually the POSitive (+) cable, is attached to the starter.

Starter Maintenance

1. Use clean fuel.
2. Tune-up the engine every YEAR.
3. Use the glow-plugs when starting a DIESEL engine.

Apply the parking brake firmly before starting the engine. Do not operate the starter for more the 10 seconds. If the engine does not start, wait at least one minute before trying again.

Testing The Starter

The starter should crank the engine easily and quickly without making any unusual noise. Do not operate the starter while the engine is running.

Repairing The Starter

If the starter does not work properly, first check to be sure the battery is fully charged and the battery cable connections are clean and tight. Repairing the starter demands special tools and training. Replacing a damaged starter, however, is relatively easy.

1. Park the car in a safe level place. Apply the parking brake. Turn the key switch to OFF.
2. Disconnect the battery (NEGative cable).
3. Label the wires connected to the starter or make a sketch so they can be easily reconnected.
4. Disconnect the wires from the starter.
5. Remove the bolts holding the starter to the engine. Then remove the starter.
6. Install the new starter. Tighten the bolts.
7. Reconnect the wires onto the new starter.
8. Reconnect the battery.

Alternator

The alternator produces electrical power needed to operate the car and keep the battery charged. It is located near the front of the engine and is turned by a belt. If the alternator breaks while the engine is running, the battery light will come ON, the ammeter will show a NEGative (-) charge, or the voltmeter will show a low voltage. You may still drive the car a short distance if there is power in the battery and no other problems. Watch the other gauges or warning lights carefully.

Older cars used a generator instead of an alternator; however, both items basically do the same thing. The alternator is used on newer cars, because it can rotate faster and keep the battery charged even at lower engine speeds.

Alternator Maintenance

1. Inspect the electrical connections on the alternator.

2. Check the condition and tension of the belt.

Keep dirt and oil out of the alternator.

Testing The Alternator

1. The electrical system indicators should not show any problem with the battery.

2. The battery should remain fully charged and able to start the engine easily.

Repairing The Alternator

Repairing the alternator demands special tools and training. Replacing a damaged alternator, however, is relatively easy. Park the car in a safe level place. Apply the parking brake. Turn the key switch OFF.

1. Disconnect the battery (NEGative cable).
2. Label the wires connected to the alternator carefully so they can be correctly reconnected.
3. Disconnect the wires from the alternator.
4. Loosen the alternator bracket.
5. Remove the alternator belt.
6. Remove the alternator.
7. Install the new alternator.
8. Replace the alternator belt.
9. Pull the alternator away from the engine in order to tighten the belt.
10. Tighten the alternator bracket.
11. Reconnect the wires onto the new alternator.
12. Reconnect the battery.

Voltage Regulator

The voltage regulator adjusts the electricity produced by the alternator to keep the battery fully charged and supply enough power to the accessories. The car may have either an internal or external voltage regulator. The internal voltage regulator is inside the alternator. The external voltage regulator is in a small metal box underneath the hood.

If the voltage regulator breaks:

1. The lights of the car may become brighter or dimmer depending on the engine speed,

2. The voltmeter may show above 16 Volts or below 10 Volts,

3. The battery may go dead and be unable to start the engine, or

4. The battery may have a very low level of battery fluid because it is overcharged.

Voltage Regulator Maintenance

The voltage regulator should be protected from water, mud, oil and excessive heat.

The external voltage regulator must be attached to a METAL part of the car.

Testing The Voltage Regulator

1. The voltmeter should indicate between 12 and 14 volts while the engine is running.

2. The battery should remain fully charged and able to start the engine easily.

Repairing The Voltage Regulator

Repairing or adjusting the voltage regulator demands special tools and training. Replacing the external voltage regulator is relatively easy.

Follow these general steps and refer to the shop manual. Park the car in a safe level place. Apply the parking brake. Turn the key switch to OFF.

1. Disconnect the battery (NEGative cable).
2. Label the wires/connectors on the voltage regulator carefully so that they can be correctly reconnected.
3. Disconnect the wires from the regulator.
4. Remove the old voltage regulator.
5. Install the new voltage regulator. Fasten it securely fastened to a METAL part of the car.
6. Reconnect the wires onto the new regulator.
7. Reconnect the battery.

Wires & Fuses

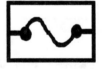

Wires transport the electrical power from the battery to the correct location in the car. The fuse is the weak link in the circuit, which breaks to prevent major damage to the electrical system. Fuses are rated in amps or the amount of electrical power needed to break them.

> Broken fuses should always be replaced with a new fuse of the same amp rating in order to protect the electrical system from damage.

Color coded wires connect the battery to the electrical accessories. The fuses are located at the fuse box under the dashboard or near the engine. The location of each wire and fuse can be found on the wiring diagram in the shop manual. A main fuse is connected to the battery.

Connectors are used to connect (or disconnect) wires quickly. Most connectors have a latch that must be pressed before the plastic parts can be pulled apart. The connector can be attached in only one position (to prevent crossing the wires). Connectors should fit together tightly and they should be protected from dirt, water, and heat.

A Short Circuit

Electrical power from the battery must make a complete circuit between the POSitive (+) and NEGative (-) terminals of the battery. If any part of the circuit (wire, fuse, connecter) is loose or broken, the accessories within that loop may not operate properly. A loose or broken wire can cause a short circuit, producing sparks, heat, or a fire. A short circuit can cause serious damage to the electrical system.

Wire & Fuse Maintenance

1. Use fuses with the correct AMP rating.

1. All wires should be protected from sharp metal edges and hot or moving car parts. Use electrical tape to wrap damaged wires or protect wires from sharp objects.

2. Cover connections, if necessary, to protect them from dirt, oil, water, or heat.

> Do not attach electrical items directly to the battery. Make connections at the fuse box so the item will be protected by a fuse.

Replacing A Fuse

Before replacing a fuse, look for the problem which caused the fuse to break. This will help avoid breaking the new fuse.

PLUG-IN FUSE   ROUND FUSE

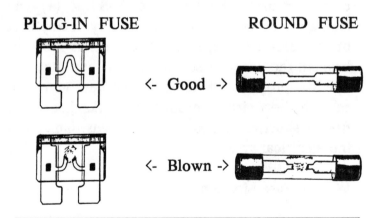

<- Good ->

<- Blown ->

> Carry an assortment of extra fuses in the tool kit and learn how to change a fuse.

FUEL SYSTEMS

Gasoline or diesel fuel stored in the fuel tank is pumped through a filter on its way to the engine. The carburetor or fuel injectors mix the fuel with air so it can be burned inside the engine. The exhaust pipes carry the burned gases away from the engine.

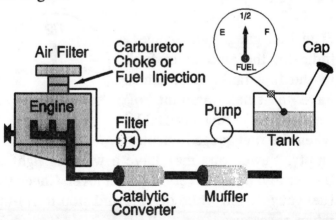

Octane

Octane refers to the fuels ability to prevent engine knock (or ping). Continuous knocking can damage the engine. High performance engines or high mileage engines may require higher octane fuels. If the engine knocks while going up a hill or when accelerating, have a tune-up. If the engine continues to knock, use a higher octane fuel. The owners manual recommends the minimum octane needed for the engine.

> High octane fuel will not provide better performance, higher MPG, or more cleaning ability. Use the fuel recommended in the owners manual.

Fuel Gauge

The fuel gauge (gas gauge), indicates the amount of fuel in the fuel tank. Most tanks have a small amount of Reserve (R) fuel available when the fuel gauge indicates empty. Newer cars may have a warning light or buzzer to indicate a very low fuel level. Check the fuel gauge often while driving and stop to fill-up, when necessary.

If the fuel gauge breaks: 1) Check the fuse box for a broken fuse, 2) Check the electrical connections at the fuel gauge and the tank to be sure they are clean and tight, and 3) Look for a broken or pinched wire somewhere between the fuel gauge and the tank.

Fuel Tank Cap

The fuel tank cap, or gas cap, does more than just prevent fuel from spilling out of the tank. The cap also prevents fuel vapors from escaping, which would cause air pollution. It keeps dirt and water from getting into the tank, while at the same time allowing air to enter the tank as the fuel is used by the engine. Never smoke or have sparks or a flame near the car while filling the fuel tank.

When removing the cap, there may be a rush of air from inside the fuel tank. This is normal and indicates that the cap is operating correctly. A locking cap or a locking door covering the cap is an inexpensive item which can prevent someone from stealing the fuel or putting the wrong type of fuel into the tank.

Do not drive a car when the fuel cap is missing. Install a new fuel cap every 4 YEARS.

Fuel Tank

The fuel tank holds a supply of the fuel needed to operate the engine. The tank has a drain plug near the bottom. The fuel tank is located away from the engine. If the car is driven on rough roads, install a skid plate under the tank to protect it from damage.

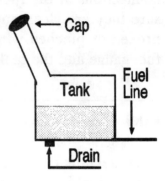

Keep the fuel tank at least 1/2 full. This reduces the chance of running out of fuel, helps prevent rust and water from forming inside the tank, and provides frequent rest stops on a long trip. Do not overfill the fuel tank. Overfilling can cause a leak. Keep sparks and heat away from the tank.

If the tank is leaking, park the car in a well ventilated area and have it repaired immediately. Special sealants can be used to plug small holes. Gasoline and diesel fuel will dissolve most types of glue and sealants. Test the sealant to be sure it will not dissolve.

An empty fuel tank can be very dangerous. Fuel vapor mixed with air can explode!

Fuel Lines

The fuel lines are small hoses which carry the fuel from the tank to the engine. These hoses are usually metal, but can also be rubber or plastic. The fuel lines are sometimes covered to protect them from damage or excessive heat. Any fuel leak is a waste of money and a dangerous fire hazard. If the fuel lines become clogged or bent, the engine may not operate properly.

Vapor Lock

Vapor lock occurs when the liquid fuel becomes very hot and small air bubbles form in the fuel lines. This can cause poor engine performance or the engine may stop.

> Remove vapor lock by carefully pouring cold water on the fuel lines. Do not get any electrical ignition parts wet.

Check underneath the car for leaks each week. Have all leaks fixed immediately. Tighten a leaky connection. Replace a damaged fuel line. Be sure the fuel lines are not near the hot exhaust pipes. Carry a small piece of fuel line and some small hose clamps in the tool kit.

Fuel Pump

The fuel pump moves the fuel from the tank to the engine. There are two types of pumps: mechanical and electrical. The mechanical pump is bolted to the side of the engine. A lever on the pump moves back and forth causing the pump to operate. The electrical pump is usually located inside the tank, but can be near the engine. The electrical pump will have two wires to provide the power from battery.

> If you run out of fuel, the electric fuel pump may overheat and be damaged.

Several fuel lines are connected to the fuel pump. The fuel line from the bottom of the tank is attached to the IN hole. The fuel line to the engine is attached to the OUT hole. Some pumps have a third By-Pass/Return hole which sends excess fuel back to the tank and helps prevent vapor lock.

Fuel Pump Maintenance

Test the fuel pump every 4 YEARS. A regular fuel pump produces about 4 PSI (2 PSI minimum). If the engine has fuel injection, the pressure is much higher (about 50 PSI).

If the pressure is good, check the output of the fuel pump. Connect one end of a rubber hose to the OUT hole on the pump and place the other end in a plastic jug. Crank the engine for several seconds to see if fuel squirts into the jug.

Most fuel pumps cannot be repaired. Replace the fuel pump according to the shop manual. Check the fuel filter(s), tank, and fuel lines before deciding to replace the pump.

Electric fuel pumps have a safety switch which turns the pump OFF in case of an accident. This switch can often be reset if accidentally bumped into the OFF position. Check the trunk area or refer to the shop manual.

Fuel Filter

Even clean fuel contains small amounts of water and dirt. The fuel filter removes these contaminants from the fuel as it is pumped to the engine. Dirty fuel is a major cause of poor engine performance and low fuel economy. It can also clog up the carburetor or injectors and cause engine damage. Fuel filters can be located in the fuel pump, carburetor, fuel tank or as a separate unit along the fuel line between the tank and engine.

Some cars have two fuel filters. One filter is for dirt particles and the other filter removes water. Fuel injected engines will have bigger and more expensive fuel filters.

Some fuel filters (water separators) have a drain plug which can be used to remove water or dirt which settles near the bottom of the filter. Do this as needed (every 2 months) or according to the owners manual.

Fuel Filter Maintenance

Replace the fuel filter(s) each YEAR. Replace the fuel filter(s) more often if the fuel supply is not clean. When the fuel filter becomes slightly clogged, the pump may not be able to supply enough fuel to the engine. The engine may operate normally at low speeds, because very little fuel is required. However, at higher speeds, when the engine needs more fuel, the engine may seem to lose power or sputter. If the fuel filter becomes blocked with dirt, the engine may stop.

The fuel filter is marked IN (from tank) and OUT (to engine) indicating the direction of fuel flow. Install the fuel filter correctly.

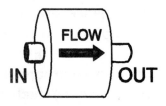

Carburetor

The carburetor located on top of the engine mixes the fuel with air so the mixture will burn easily inside the engine. A rich fuel-air mixture has more fuel (less air), which produces more power and makes the engine turn faster. A rich mixture is needed to start a cold engine and when driving up a hill. A lean fuel-air mixture has less fuel (more air), which produces less power and allows the engine to turn slowly. A lean mixture is used when the engine is idling and while cruising at a constant speed.

A carburetor is sensitive to changes in altitude. If the carburetor is adjusted correctly for driving near the ocean, it may not operate very good when driving in the mountains.

Carburetor Maintenance

Check the fuel economy of the engine (MPG) every 2 MONTHS. Clean the carburetor inside and out with a spray carburetor/choke cleaner every 6 MONTHS. Most newer carburetors are preset at the factory and need no adjustments. If adjustments or repairs are needed, be sure to follow the instructions in the shop manual.

Carburetor Icing

When the weather is cool and wet, ice can form inside the carburetor and cause poor engine performance. Heat from the engine should keep the carburetor warm and prevent carburetor icing. The ice will melt when the engine warms up.

Carburetor icing is seldom a problem in very cold weather. It happens most often in cool damp weather.

Carburetor Repairs

Hopefully, cleaning the carburetor will make the car run good normally. If the carburetor has been damaged by dirt and water, it must be repaired, rebuilt, or replaced.

A remanufactured carburetor may be available, which is an old carburetor that has been professionally cleaned and rebuilt to like-new condition.

Rebuild kits are available for most carburetors. These kits contain most of the parts necessary to repair a damaged carburetor. Be sure it contains both a float and the float valve. If necessary, purchase these parts separately.

Fuel Injection

Fuel injection is another way to mix the fuel and air together before it is burned in the engine. Fuel injection sprays the fuel directly into the engine where it mixes with the air and burns. The fuel injection system consist of both the fuel injection pump and the injectors. The injection system must provide the proper quantity of fuel at the right time to allow the engine to operate properly. Fuel injection can be used on either gasoline or diesel fuel engines. Dirt and water in the fuel can damage the injection pump and clog the injectors.

Fuel Injection Maintenance

Always use clean fuel and replace the fuel filter(s) regularly. If the fuel injection system has been damaged by dirt and water, it must be repaired or replaced.

Do not run out of fuel when driving a fuel injected car. If air enters the injection pump, the engine will stop and it may not restart even after more fuel is added to the tank.

Fuel injector cleaners are available, but are not normally needed. Most gasoline contains adequate cleaning additives. If you choose to use additional cleaners, add them to a FULL tank of fuel.

Fuel Pedal

The fuel pedal (gas pedal, accelerator) controls the amount of fuel (or air) entering the engine. This determines the speed and power of the engine. The pedal is connected to either the carburetor or fuel injection with a linkage system consisting of cables, levers, and springs.

While driving, keep the position of the fuel pedal as steady as possible and make changes slowly to maximize the fuel economy and life of the engine. Cruise control automatically adjust the position of the pedal to maintain a constant minimum car speed.

If the fuel pedal squeaks or become sticky, lubricate the fuel pedal linkage with a can of spray oil. If the pedal is slippery, remove the rubber pad and apply a mixture of epoxy cement and small rocks to the pedal surface.

Choke

The choke (carburetor engines) is used to adjust the fuel-air mixture to provide a rich mixture (more fuel) when the engine is cold. The choke should be closed when the cold engine starts and then slowly opened as the engine warms up. The automatic choke, is set by pressing the fuel pedal one time before starting the engine and adjust automatically depending on the engine temperature. The choke is usually not needed unless the engine is cold (below 50F).

If the choke does not close properly, the engine may not start. If the choke does not open as the engine warms up, the engine may lack power, use more fuel (lower MPG), and the exhaust gases may be black.

The engine should start easily, even in cold weather. It should also run smoothly and get normal fuel economy (MPG). If not, the choke may need to be adjusted or repaired. A stuck choke is a common problem. Clean the choke with a spray carburetor/choke cleaner every 6 MONTHS. Follow the directions provided with the cleaner.

Air Filter

The engine needs both fuel and air. In fact, for every one gallon of fuel burned, the engine needs about 10,000 gallons of air. The air filter cleans the air before it is mixed with the fuel.

A **paper filter** is the most common type used on cars. This filter is inexpensive, but should be replaced regularly. A **foam filter** is sometimes used in very dusty conditions as a pre-filter (before the air passes through the paper filter). The foam filter can, however, be washed and used several times.

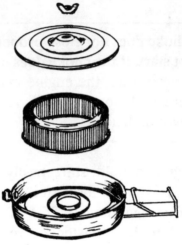

The air filter is located on top of the carburetor or near the engine. The preheat valve is on the intake section of the air filter.

Preheat Valve

Both very cold air and very hot air will reduce the engine performance. On cold days, the air entering the filter is preheated by the hot exhaust pipes. The preheat valve adjusts automatically, depending on the air temperature, to supply the engine with warm air.

When driving in warm weather, the preheat valve should be closed to prevent very hot air from entering the air filter.

Air Filter Maintenance

Replace the paper air filter every YEAR. Be sure the air filter housing is securely attached to the engine to prevent unfiltered air from entering the engine. Do not drive a car without an air filter. This could damage the engine and cause a fire. Do not allow water to enter the air filter when driving through deep water. This will damage the engine.

A dirty or clogged air filter will cause poor engine performance and low MPG because not enough air can be mixed with the fuel. A damaged air filter may allow dirt to get inside the carburetor or engine causing damage.

If you replace the air filter once a year, do not worry about testing it. If the filter looks dirty, however, change it. Do not use compressed air to clean a paper air filter. Do not reuse the old filter.

Turbocharger

A turbocharger (turbo) is a small air compressor used to force air into the engine. If more air is pushed into the engine, more fuel can be used, and therefore, more power is produced. The turbo is turned by the hot exhaust gases leaving the engine. The turbo will increase both the power produced by the engine and the fuel economy (more MPG).

The turbocharger must rotate very fast and, therefore, the extra power is available only at higher engine speeds (high RPMs). The turbo is located on the engine near the exhaust pipes and is connected to the air filter. Although a turbo may enhance the performance of the engine, it is not usually necessary for normal driving conditions and requires extra maintenance and repair cost.

The major benefit from using a turbocharger is obtaining more power or providing better engine performance. However, unless weight, size, and performance are extremely important, a larger non-turbocharger engine may be less expensive to buy and maintain.

A supercharger is very similar to a turbocharger, except that it is rotated by a belt with power from the engine. A supercharger will also increase the power produced by the engine, but it will reduce the fuel economy (lower MPG).

Turbocharger Maintenance

After a long trip, allow a turbocharged engine to idle for about one minute before turning the key switch to OFF. This allows the engine oil to circulate and cool the turbocharger. Use a good quality engine oil with the proper viscosity (thickness) and change the oil and filter regularly. The most common turbocharger problem is damage to the bearings because of inadequate lubrication or excessive heat.

When driving a turbocharged car, the engine will produce more power at higher engine speeds (above 3000 RPM) when the turbocharger kicks-in. A turbo-gauge may be installed on the dashboard to indicate correct turbocharger operation.

Most engines pull the fuel-air mixture into the cylinders with vacuum. A turbo, however, forces the fuel-air mixture into the engine under pressure. Use caution when using a vacuum gauge on a turbocharger engine. The increased pressure from the turbocharger may damage the gauge.

Exhaust Pipes & Muffler

The exhaust pipes and muffler carry the hot exhaust gases away from the engine. Burning the fuel-air mixture 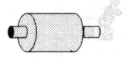 inside the engine produces heat, noise, and exhaust gases. Some of the heat is absorbed by the radiator fluid or the engine oil, but most of the heat remains in the exhaust gases. The noise from the engine is reduced by the muffler, which contains the exhaust gases until they can expand gases are not only very hot, but they contain poisonous substances. Many newer cars also have emission controls as part of the exhaust system to reduce the amount of air pollution.

> Water is part of the exhaust gases. Drops of water or steam may be visible from the exhaust pipe outlet when you start the engine.

Do not operate a car in an enclosed area without adequate ventilation. The poisonous exhaust gases can cause drowsiness, a headache, or even death. Do not park the car in tall grass or over flammable objects. The exhaust pipes are very hot and can cause a fire.

Exhaust Pipe Maintenance

Check for damage to the exhaust system, such as a loose pipe or increased engine noise each WEEK. Have the exhaust pipes and muffler checked for leaks or damage as part of the annual inspection or tune-up. Repair or replace these parts, as needed.

Unleaded fuel and proper emission controls will help the exhaust system to last a long time. If the exhaust system is clogged, the engine may lack power, backfire, or stop. The exhaust pipes can become clogged with dirt or rust.

ENGINES

The fuel-air mixture burns inside the engine to produce power needed to move the car and keep the engine running. Oil lubricates, cleans, and cools the moving parts inside the engine. Belts are used to turn the water pump, alternator, power steering pump, air conditioner compressor, etc.

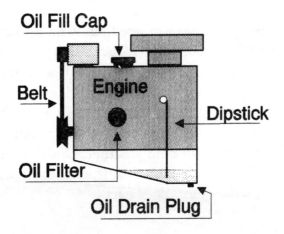

Gasoline & Diesel Engines

The primary difference between a gasoline and
diesel engine is how the fuel-air mixture is ignited
inside the engine, or in other words the ignition
system. A gasoline engine uses an electric spark
from the sparkplug. The diesel engine injects fuel
directly into the engine, causing it to ignite with
the very hot air.

A gasoline engine will always have sparkplugs.

A gasoline engine is light weight, has good
performance, quicker acceleration, and is less
expensive to service and repair. However, the
gasoline engine will need more frequent
adjustments, more expensive fuel, and cannot
operate when wet.

A diesel engine does not need many adjustments,
gets better fuel economy (higher MPG), uses less
expensive fuel, operates longer without major
repairs, operates in very wet conditions, and has
very good pulling power (torque). However, it is
heavy, more expensive to service and repair, and
very hard to start in cold weather. Diesel engines
also sound and smell like big trucks, even when
they are used in passenger cars.

Engine Valves & Cylinder Head Bolts

The engine has valves which allow the fuel-air mixture to enter the engine and the exhaust gases to leave the engine.

Newer cars have **multi-valve engines**, or more than two valves per cylinder. These engine can produce more power and better fuel economy (higher MPG); however, they cost more to purchase, maintain, and repair.

Hydraulic valves are adjusted automatically with the oil pressure inside the engine. Manual valves should be checked about every six months.

Cylinder head bolts hold the top part of the engine in place. These bolts should be checked every six months to be sure they stay tight. A torque wrench is needed to tighten to the specifications found in the shop manual. If these bolts become loose, the head gasket can be damaged and cause the engine to loose power or leak radiator fluid.

Compression Test

A compression test can be used to check the internal condition of the engine, without actually taking the engine apart. A compression gauge, actually a special air pressure gauge, is connected to each sparkplug hole in order to measure the compression inside the cylinder. Low compression can indicate damaged valves, internal engine wear, or a blown head gasket.

Tachometer

A tachometer indicates the engine speed, or in other words, how fast the parts inside of the engine are turning in Revolutions Per Minute (RPM).

The engine is designed to operate between a slowest speed (idle) and a fastest speed (redline). Lower engine speeds should be used when less power is needed, such cruising at a steady speed or going downhill. Higher engine speeds are needed to produce more power for accelerating, going up a hill, or carrying heavy loads. The speed of the engine is controlled by moving the fuel pedal.

Drive with moderate engine speeds between 2000 to 4000 RPMs (1000 to 2500 for diesel engines). Do not lug the engine (drive with a very low engine speed) or allow the engine to speed up to the redline.

RPM = Revolutions Per Minute (Engine Speed)

Vacuum Gauge

The vacuum gauge can be useful in determining the fuel economy (MPG) and several common engine problems. Vacuum, or suction, is created when parts inside the engine pull the fuel-air mixture into the engine.

A vacuum gauge can be attached to the engine for a quick engine diagnosis or permanently installed on the dashboard of the car for reference when needed. All vacuum line connections must be tight in order to prevent unfiltered air from entering the engine.

Low vacuum indicates poor fuel economy or low MPG, when more fuel is being used by the engine. High vacuum indicates very little fuel is being used or good fuel economy (high MPG).

The vacuum gauge measures Inches of Mercury, sometimes called Inches of Vacuum or just Inches. Higher altitudes will cause a slightly lower vacuum reading. Vacuum is used operate the cruise control, emission controls, and adjust the ignition system . See also Chapter 6 - Spark Advance.

Using The Vacuum Gauge

1. When the engine is warm and running at idle speed, the vacuum gauge pointer should be steady - between 15 and 22 Inches.

2. When the engine is warm and running at idle speed, press the fuel pedal quickly and then release it. The vacuum gauge pointer should drop quickly, then rise above normal, and finally, return to the normal position.

If the vacuum gauge readings are low or the pointer vibrates when the engine is at idle speed, the engine needs to be adjusted or repaired. Check the engine timing, leaking gaskets, engine valves, and exhaust system.

Lubricating Systems

Lubrication provides a slippery surface between two or more parts in order to reduce friction, remove heat, and avoid damage. Lubrication depends on both the parts rubbing together and the force between the parts. Engine oil needs the most frequent service, because the parts inside the engine are very hot and dirty. However, the transmission, differential, steering box, chassis parts, cooling system, steering system, and car body also need proper lubrication.

Viscosity

All lubricants (engine oil) are classified according to the viscosity or thickness (weight). The higher numbers are thicker oils. SAE 50 (thick) oil is often recommended for the engine in hot weather. Thinner oil, SAE 20, can be used in cold weather. Differential oil may be SAE 90 and therefore, is much thicker than engine oil. Some oils have special additives which enable them to operate in both hot and cold weather. SAE 10W-40 is a multi-weight oil, where "W" indicates approval for Winter use.

Use a lubricant recommended by the owners manual. The API rating indicates the quality of the oil. Current rating are SG for gasoline engines and CE for diesel engines. Newer and better oil will be rated SH and CF. If the oil is rated "Energy Conserving", it has slippery additives to reduce friction.

All the information you need (API Service Rating, Viscosity, and Energy Conserving) can be found on the round symbol.

Do not mix different types of lubricants. Poor quality lubricants or different types of lubricants mixed together can cause damage. Store lubricants in tightly sealed containers.

If lubrication is neglected, excessive heat and friction will cause parts to wear-out quickly and they will need to be replaced more often.

Special engine oil additives are not necessary if a high quality oil is used and the oil and filter changed often.

Oil Pressure Indicators

Oil is circulated inside the engine to lubricate, cool, and clean many different moving parts. The oil pressure indicator warns you if there is not adequate pressure. It can be either a warning light or pressure gauge. The warning light is easy to see; however, the oil pressure gauge gives a more accurate indication of the lubricating system.

Observe the oil pressure indicator each time the engine starts and frequently while driving to be sure the engine oil is lubricating properly. Allow the engine to idle (less than 2000 RPM) for about 10 seconds each time it starts. The oil pump needs a few seconds to get the engine oil circulating properly. High engine speed can cause damage.

When the oil pressure is very LOW, the engine will make clicking sounds.

The oil pressure light should be
ON when the key switch is turned
to the ON position. The light
should go OFF when the engine
starts indicating that the engine
has the minimum oil pressure
needed.

The oil pressure gauge
indicates the exact
pressure in the engine
lubricating system. The oil
pressure can vary
depending on the
temperature and speed of
the engine. The pressure
will be higher when the

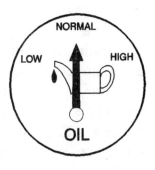

engine is cold or turning fast. The pressure may be
lower when the engine is warm or turning slowly.

If the oil pressure drops very LOW, or the oil
light come ON, stop the car and turn the engine
OFF to avoid serious engine damage. Low oil
pressure can be caused by a low level of engine
oil, improper type of engine oil, oil that has been
diluted by fuel or water, damage inside the engine,
or a faulty oil by-pass valve.

> Low oil pressure can cause serious engine
> damage in a few minutes.

Oil Filter

The oil filter cleans the oil as it circulates in the engine. Oil collects dirt and burned fuel particles from inside the engine. These contaminants must be removed by the oil filter in order to prevent engine damage. The filter on most cars is a single unit containing both the paper filter (inside) and the  metal container (outside). This type of filter is simply screwed onto the engine. Some cars have a two-piece filter, consisting of a replaceable paper filter inside a reusable metal container. The oil filter is located near the bottom or on the side of the engine.

Replace the oil and filter every 2 MONTHS. Even if you do not drive your car very much at all, change the oil four times a year: spring, summer, fall and winter. The oil filter should be replaced every time the engine oil is changed. Do not put clean oil into a dirty oil filter.

If you decide not to change the oil and filter yourself, be sure the mechanic installs good quality oil and filter. Purchase several oil drain plug washers at the dealership so you will have one for the mechanic to use.

Changing The Oil and Filter

1. Park the car in a safe level place. Apply the parking brake. Run the engine for several minutes, then turn the engine OFF.

2. Place a flat bucket (two gallon) underneath the oil drain plug. Remove the oil drain plug on the bottom of the engine to allow the dirty oil to drain out. **Caution!** HOT oil will come out when the drain plug is removed.

3. Use an oil filter wrench to remove the dirty oil filter. Turn the filter Counter-Clock-Wise. **Caution!** The filter is full of HOT oil.

4. Apply some oil to the rubber gasket on the new oil filter. This allows the filter to be tighten properly and prevents leaks.

5. Install the new oil filter. Tighten the filter by hand. Check for instructions on the oil filter. Do not overtighten the filter, which can damage the filter and cause leaks.

6. After all of the old dirty oil drains out of the engine, install a new gasket on the drain plug. Replace the plug and tighten it securely.

7. Check the filter and drain plug to be sure both are installed correctly.

8. Check the owners manual to determine how much oil should be added to the engine. Remove the oil fill cap and use a funnel to pour most (not all) of the oil into the engine.

9. Check the oil level using the dipstick. Add more oil until the dipstick indicates a FULL level. Do not overfill.

10. Replace the dipstick and fill cap.

11. Start the engine and allow it to idle for several minutes. If the oil pressure indicator does not show adequate engine oil pressure within 15 seconds, turn the engine OFF.

12. After one minute, turn the engine OFF and check the oil level using the dipstick. Add more engine oil, if necessary, until the dipstick indicates the FULL level. Do not overfill.

Dispose of the dirty oil properly. If possible, return it to be recycled.

Oil Dipstick

Use the dipstick to check the oil level. For an accurate reading, the car must be level and the engine OFF. Near the bottom of the dipstick are two marks. The upper mark indicates the FULL (maximum) oil level. The lower mark indicates the ADD (minimum) oil level. The distance between the two marks represents one quart of oil.

Do not operate the engine when the oil level is above the FULL mark or below the ADD mark.

The Dipstick

Check the engine oil level each WEEK. Add more clean oil, as needed, to maintain a FULL level. Do not overfill.

1. Park the car in a safe level place. Apply the parking brakes. Turn the engine OFF. Wait about one minute. This allows the oil to drain back into the bottom of the oil pan.

Chapter 5

2. Remove the dipstick and wipe it clean.
3. Replace the dipstick.
4. Remove it again and check the oil level.
5. Replace the dipstick.

Oil Fill Cap & Drain Plug

Clean oil is added to the engine through the hole under the oil fill cap. Dirty oil is drained by removing the oil drain plug on the bottom of the engine. Use a funnel to avoid spilling oil onto the engine. Install a new gasket on the drain plug at each oil change.

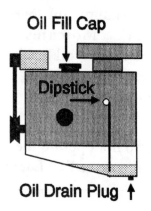

Belts

The engine uses flexible rubber belts, fan belts, or V-Belts, to turn items needed to operate the car. Each belt sits inside several round pulleys. The large pulley near the bottom of the engine turns when the parts inside the engine turn. This large pulley turns the belts, which turn the other smaller pulleys. These smaller pulleys can be connected to the radiator fan, water pump, alternator, vacuum pump, A/C compressor, power steering pump, etc. The belts are near the front of the engine. Newer cars may have one long belt (serpentine belt) which operates on all the pulleys.

An **idler pulley** is not connected to anything, but is used to adjust the tension or position of the belt(s).

Timing Belt

There is another belt (or chain) called the timing belt on the engine. The timing belt controls the engine valves, ignition timing, or injection pump. The timing belt is inside the engine and is usually self-adjusting.

If the timing belt breaks while the engine is running, serious engine damage may occur.

Belt Maintenance

Before attempting any test or adjustments to the engine, be sure the car is parked in a safe level place and turn the engine OFF. Allow the engine to cool down, if necessary.

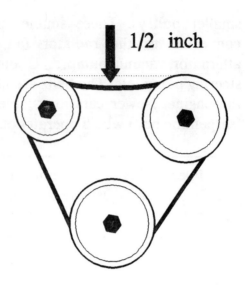

2 Push down on the belt between two pulleys. It should move down about 1/2 inch. Otherwise, adjust the tension.

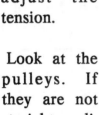

Look at the pulleys. If they are not straight or aligned properly, something is bent and needs to be repaired or replaced. Inspect the belts carefully. If the belt is cracked, has exposed strings, or shinny areas, replace it.Belts are available in many different sizes. Be sure both the length and cross-section of the belt are correct.

Check the belts every 2 MONTHS. Adjust the tension, when necessary. Inspect the timing belt (chain) each YEAR. Change all of the belts, including the timing belt, every 4 YEARS.

> If the belt squeaks or slips, tighten it.

If a belt is loose, it can slip. A slipping belt will make a screeching sound and be damaged. It may also cause the engine to overheat, run poorly, the battery may become discharged, the power steering may lack power, or the A/C may not cool. If the belt is too tight, it can break or damage the pulleys. If the pulleys are not aligned correctly, the belt may break.

Replacing A Belt

Park the car in a safe level place. Turn the engine OFF.

1. Loosen the idler puller or the adjusting bracket. There may be a locking-nut and adjusting-nut. If so, loosen the locking-nut before turning the adjusting-nut.

2. Move the pulley or bracket towards the engine in order to loosen the damaged belt. Remove the damaged belt.

3. Install the new belt and position it onto the pulleys correctly. It may be necessary to remove other belts to install the new belt.

4. Adjust the tension of the new belt by moving the bracket or pulley away from the engine. When the belt is tight, tighten the locking-nut.

New belts will stretch. Check the tension of the belt the next day and tighten it, if necessary.

Gaskets

A gasket is a soft material used between two parts to prevent leaks. Gaskets keep both liquids and gases from either escaping or entering. They provide a good seal and also can be used to position parts correctly (the thickness of the gasket can be important). Paper gaskets are common. However, some gaskets are made of rubber or metal. A round rubber gasket is called an O-ring. O-rings usually fit inside a grove and are squeezed in order to provide a good seal. A rubber O-ring is commonly used on the oil filter. Metal gaskets (washers) may be used on the oil drain plug or sparkplugs.

Be sure that both the size and material of the gasket are correct for the intended use. Do not spray high pressure water or air directly at a gasket, which can damage the gasket or allow water or air to get inside the car parts and cause damage. If a gasket leaks, it should be tightened or replaced.

Gasket sealer is sometimes needed when installing a new gasket. The sealer is a type of glue which helps hold the gasket in place and provides a better seal. Refer to the shop manual for more information.

IGNITION SYSTEMS

The electrical ignition system used in a gasoline engine provides the spark for the sparkplugs. This spark is needed to ignite the fuel-air mixture inside the engine. The distributor sends the sparks to the proper sparkplug at the right time.

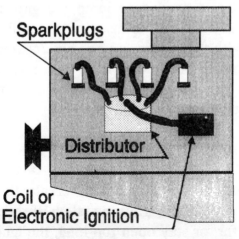

Sparkplugs

Distributor

Coil or
Electronic Ignition

An easy test for any electrical ignition system is to **look** at the engine while it is running in a dark place. Do not touch any hot or moving car parts. Small visible sparks indicate an electrical leak which can cause poor engine performance.

Standard Ignition Systems

A standard ignition system consist of three basic parts: coil, points, and condenser. Most newer cars use an electronic ignition system. (Refer to the next section in this chapter.)

Coil

The coil (a coil of wire) acts like a small voltage transformer. It boost the low voltage in the battery from 12 volts to around 20,000 volts. This very high voltage is needed to jump the gap on the sparkplugs. The coil is usually a small black cylinder with three wires on one end located near the engine. The larger wire from the center of the coil looks like a sparkplug wire and is connected to the distributor.

Points

The points open and close to create the high voltage charge in the ignition system. If the points open too far, or stay open too long, the ignition system may not work properly. The points are located inside the distributor, underneath the rotor.

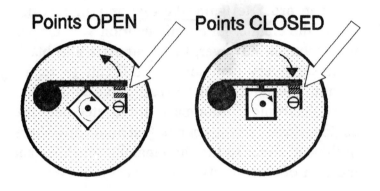

Condenser

The condenser acts as an "electrical spring" to absorb some of the shock and prevent damage to the ignition system (points). The condenser is a small silver cylinder attached to the distributor and the points.

Replace the points and condenser and adjust the engine timing every 6 MONTHS. Tune-up the engine once every YEAR.

Keep the ignition parts dry and be sure all electrical connections are clean and tight.

Electronic Ignition Systems

The newer electronic ignition systems produces a spark in order to ignite the fuel and air mixture inside the engine. Electronic ignition systems are very reliable; however, the computers and black boxes are very complex and difficult to repair without special training and expensive equipment. Most electronic ignition parts are located near the engine. However, they can be just about anywhere in the car. Refer to the shop manual for the exact location of these parts.

> Keep the electronic ignition parts dry. Be sure all electrical connections are clean and tight.

If the ignition system is damaged or not adjusted properly, the engine may not start easily or run smoothly. The engine may lack power and the fuel economy (MPG) may be low.

Advantages Of Electronic Ignition

A car with an electronic ignition system needs fewer adjustments and can operate for many years before needing to be replaced. These parts, however, usually require special testing tools, cannot be adjusted, and are very expensive to replace.

Distributor

The distributor sends, or distributes, the sparks from the ignition system to the sparkplugs. It is located either on the side or top of the engine. The two basic parts of the distributor are the distributor cap and rotor.

Distributor Cap

The distributor cap is the top part of the distributor. The center wire on the distributor cap is connected to the ignition system (coil). The wires around the outside of the distributor cap are connected to the sparkplugs. The cap must be removed to inspect the rotor. The cap is held in place with two small screws or spring clips.

The distributor cap can be assembled in only one position in order to maintain the correct alignment of the sparkplug wires. Each wire on the cap is assigned to a specific sparkplug, therefore, do not switch the position of the wires. Move the wires one at a time from the old cap to the new cap.

Rotor

The rotor turns, or rotates, inside the distributor when the engine is running in order to send the spark to the correct sparkplug at the right time.

The rotor is found inside the distributor (underneath the distributor cap). The rotor can be installed in only one position. Keep the distributor dry. Replace the cap and rotor each YEAR.

In an emergency situation, clean the corrosion off of the cap and rotor with sandpaper or a small file. Removing some of the corrosion may allow these parts to operate for a short while, but they will need to be replaced very soon.

Spark Advance

The spark advance makes very small adjustments to the engine timing (while the engine is running) so the spark will arrive at the sparkplugs sooner when the engine is turning faster. This provides the smoothest engine operation and best engine performance. There are several types of spark advances which can be used on the engine.

Vacuum Advance

If the distributor has a small rubber hose connected to it, vacuum is used to advance the timing. As the engine speeds up, changes in vacuum (suction) from the engine adjust the timing. Be sure the rubber hose is not bent, broken, or loose.

Centrifugal Advance

The centrifugal advance uses a small pair of weights which turn inside the distributor while the engine is running. As the engine speeds up, the weights spin faster and move towards the outside of the distributor. This adjust the timing of the engine. The small weights are located inside the distributor. Be sure the weights move freely and any springs are in place.

Electronic Advance

Newer cars with electronic ignition systems may
have the electronic advance built into one of the
computers or black boxes. Refer to the shop
manual for more information.

Regardless of the type of advance on your car,
have an engine tune-up each year. If the spark
advance does not work correctly, the engine
may operate smoothly at one speed (idle), but
very rough at higher engine speeds.

Sparkplug Wires

The sparkplug wires carry the spark from the
distributor to each of the sparkplugs. Each wire
has a specific hole on the distributor cap so that
the spark will arrive at the correct sparkplug at
the right time in order to ignite the fuel-air
mixture inside the engine. There is one other
similar wire which is connects the distributor cap
to the ignition system. These wires plug into the
distributor cap and onto the top of the sparkplugs.

Keep the sparkplug wires dry. Be sure each wire
is fastened securely. Keep the wires away from hot
or moving parts. Replace the sparkplug wires
about every 4 or 5 years. If a sparkplug wire is
damaged, the engine may not start easily or run

smoothly. The engine may lack power and the fuel economy (MPG) may be low. Visual inspections do not always reveal damage to a sparkplug wires. The wire may be broken on the inside.

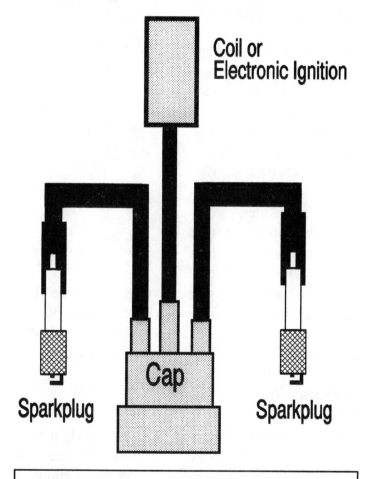

Coil or
Electronic Ignition

Cap

Sparkplug

Sparkplug

Purchase sparkplug wires in complete sets including the wire to connect the distributor to the coil. Install one wire at a time to be sure each wire is connected properly.

Sparkplugs

Sparkplugs produce the
spark which causes the
fuel-air mixture to burn
and produce the power
needed to keep the
engine running and
move the car. Each
sparkplug has two
separate metal parts.
The center part of the
sparkplug is connected
to the sparkplug wire.
The lower part of the
sparkplug touches the
engine. On the bottom

Gap

of the sparkplug (inside the engine), there is a
small gap between these two metal parts. When
the high voltage electrical charge travels from the
distributor, it jumps this gap, causing a spark.

Sparkplug Gap

The gap on the sparkplug must be the right size
to produce a good spark. The recommended gap
can be found in the owners manual, shop manual,
or underneath the hood. If the gap is given as a
minimum and maximum value, set the gap at the
minimum value.

Use a **round wire** tool to measure the gap. Flat feeler gauges may not be accurate. Never bend the center part of the sparkplug, carefully bend the outer tab to adjust the gap.

Sparkplugs are available in many different types (heat range) and sizes. Always use the correct type and size of sparkplug. If the owners manual or shop manual is not available, check the decal on the bottom of the hood or use the type of sparkplug found in the engine. If the location of the sparkplugs is not obvious, find the distributor. Follow the sparkplug wires to each sparkplug.

Replacing Sparkplugs

Before removing a sparkplug, clean around the sparkplug in order to prevent dirt from falling into the engine. When installing a sparkplug, use your hand to start the sparkplug into the hole correctly. Replace the sparkplugs each YEAR. Do not over-tighten sparkplugs, which can damage the engine or the sparkplug.

Old sparkplugs should be a light brown color. Black deposits on the sparkplug could indicate a dirty air filter or stuck choke. Oily plugs can indicate internal engine wear. If the sparkplug has been burned, adjust the engine timing.

Tune-Up

A tune-up is adjusting or making minor repairs to
the engine so that it will start easily, run smoothly,
and have normal fuel economy (MPG). A tune-up
is not a panacea for all engine problems nor
should it involve expensive major repairs. Several
tune-up items are very simple and easy to do;
however, other items require special training and
tools.

> Every engine should have an annual tune-up.
> Newer cars may need less adjustments,
> however, if you neglect the simple
> maintenance, the engine may need expensive

Watch out for the "Spark-Plugs Only" Tune-Up.
Installing new sparkplugs is probably the most
important item on the list. It is also one of the
easiest and least expensive items. Other items will
be checked, but extra charges will apply if parts or
labor are needed.

Check the tire pressure before and after the tune-
up. A few repair shops overinflate the tires so you
will get better fuel economy (MPG) and credit the
tune-up. Driving on overinflated tires might give
better MPG, but it can wear out the tires and is
dangerous.

Tune-Up

Although the following list seems long, it should cost between $75 and $150 for most cars, parts and labor included. Newer cars will use more expensive parts, but have fewer adjustments needed.

1. New Air Filter
2. New Fuel Filter(s)
3. New PCV Valve and Filter
4. New Cap, Rotor, (Points, Condenser)
5. New Sparkplugs (Check Gap)
6. Compression Test (optional)
7. Adjust Valves (not Hydraulic type)
8. Check the Timing Belt
9. Inspect the Vacuum Lines
10. Adjust the Carburetor or Fuel Injection
11. Adjust the Timing
12. Adjust the Idle Speed and Choke
13. Test the Exhaust Gases
14. Road Test the car
15. Return all the Old Parts for Inspection

Anything less, is not a real tune-up. Anything more, might be considered a repair job. The first nine items on the list are easy to do with only simple tools. Testing and adjusting the engine, if necessary, normally requires special training and tools. The tune-up should be done just prior to the annual state inspection to be sure the exhaust gases are within acceptable limits.

Glow Plugs

A cold diesel engine is very hard to start. Glow plugs are little electric heaters needed to warm the air inside the engine, so the engine can start easier. Once the engine starts, glow plugs are not needed. Use the glow plugs for about 15 seconds before turning the key switch to the START position. In very cold weather, or when the battery is weak, allow the glow plugs to operate longer.

Use the glow plugs each time you start a diesel engine. If the glow plugs are broken or not used, the engine will be harder to start or it may not start at all. If the glow plugs do not work, check the fuse box.

In an emergency situation it may be possible to supply power from the battery directly to the glow plugs in order to start the engine. Connect one end of a jumper cable (large wire) to the POSitive (+) terminal of the battery. Carefully touch the other end to the cable to the top of one of the glow plugs. Hold this connection for about 30 seconds. Then remove the jumper cable and try to start the engine.

COOLING SYSTEMS

Heat produced by the engine must be constantly removed to avoid overheating. Radiator fluid is pumped from the engine to the radiator to maintain a constant temperature. This hot radiator fluid is also used for the heater system. The thermostat controls the flow of radiator fluid to maintain a normal engine operating temperature.

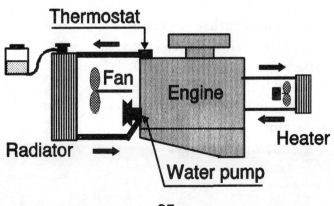

Engine Temperature Indicators

The engine must be warm to run properly and efficiently. A cold engine wastes fuel. A very hot engine will overheat. Engine temperature indicators allows you to easily monitor the engine temperature. Your car should have either a temperature warning light or gauge.

Warning Light

The temperature warning light should always be OFF, indicating that the engine temperature is below a critical level.

If your car has a COLD temperature warning light, it should come ON until the engine temperature warms up. Then it should go OFF.

Temperature Gauge

The temperature gauge displays the engine temperature between COLD (C) and HOT (H). The normal engine operating temperature is usually near the middle of the gauge.

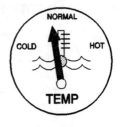

If the engine overheats, turn the A/C **OFF** and the heater **ON**. Stop the car and allow the engine to idle for **one minute**. If the engine does not cool down, turn the engine **OFF**.

If the temperature indicators do not work properly, check the fuse box. Also check for loose electrical connections at the engine or dashboard.

Radiator Fluid

Most of the heat produced inside the engine leaves with the exhaust gases. The radiator fluid absorbs excess heat from the engine and transfers it to the radiator where the heat can be released to the outside air. Radiator fluid should be a mixture of water and coolant (anti-freeze). This prevents the engine from overheating, protects against rust, lubricates the water pump, and keeps the cooling system from freezing in very cold weather.

Radiator fluid is very poisonous, even though it has a sweet taste. Keep it away from children and animals.

Check the amount of radiator fluid in the expansion tank each WEEK. Add clean water in order to maintain the FULL level. Do not fill above the HOT (FULL) level, which could cause a spill when the engine warms up.

The radiator fluid should be light green. If the fluid is brown or over 2 years old, flush the system and change the fluid. Flush-N-Fill kits are available at most auto parts store which simplifies changing the radiator fluid. Follow the directions provided with the kit.

Add a can of **Rust Inhibitor & Water Pump Lubricant** after 1 YEAR and change the radiator fluid every 2 YEARS. Use a 50/50 mixture (equal parts of clean water and coolant) Warning: using pure coolant as radiator fluid will cause the engine to overheat.

A special tool can test the radiator fluid to determine the approximate freezing point. This test is not accurate or necessary if you replace the radiator fluid every 2 years.

Radiator

The radiator transfers heat from the fluid to the air. The radiator is a large metal box containing many small tubes. Air blows through the radiator and absorbs heat from the fluid. The thin pieces of metal between the small tubes help disperse the heat quickly. The drain valve located near the bottom of the radiator can be used to remove the radiator fluid. The expansion tank is connected to the radiator with a small rubber hose.

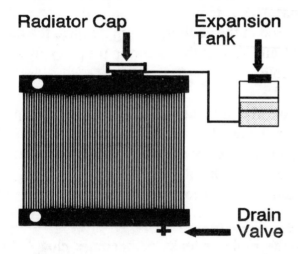

A radiator can be any device used to transfer heat from one substance to another. Normally, it refers to the engine radiator. A car may also have an engine oil radiator (oil cooler), A/C radiators, heater radiator, and transmission radiator (A/T cooler).

An engine oil cooler or automatic transmission cooler can be purchased at most car parts stores. Cars driven in hot climates or used to pull heavy loads should have such a cooler installed.

Check for radiator for leaks. A small hole may leak only when the engine is hot. Look for a whitish deposits on the radiator or listen for hissing sounds when the engine is hot. Special additives are available to stop small leaks in the radiator as a temporary repair. If these additives are used in the cooling system, replace the radiator fluid and repair the radiator properly as soon as possible.

Clean the outside of the radiator by spraying water from the engine side out, or carefully removing debris from the front of the radiator. Do not bend or damage the small metal fins which would prevent proper air flow.

If the radiator leaks or becomes clogged with rust (inside) or leaves and bugs (outside), the engine may overheat and be damaged.

If the radiator is loose, tighten the bolts or replace the rubber bushings. A loose radiator may vibrate or hit the fan, causing damage or leaks. If the radiator is leaking, remove the radiator and have the hole soldered closed.

Radiator Cap

The radiator cap does more than just cover the top of the radiator and prevent the radiator fluid from spilling. As the engine warms up, the radiator fluid actually expands. The radiator cap allows some pressure to build up inside the radiator. Excess radiator fluid drains out of the radiator and into the expansion tank. A pressurized cooling system cools the engine better and prevents the radiator

fluid from boiling. When the engine cools down, the radiator cap allows some of the excess radiator fluid stored in the expansion tank to be syphoned back into the radiator. The cap is on top of the radiator.

Do not remove or touch the radiator cap when the engine is **HOT**. The cap will be very hot and steam may burn you.

Replace the radiator cap every 4 YEARS (when the engine is COLD). Push down on the cap and turn it slowly Counter Clock Wise or to the left. If you hear a hissing sound, release the cap and wait for the noise to stop. Carefully remove the old cap. Install the new cap by pressing down and turning it Clock Wise or to the right.

If there is a very small leak in the cooling system, loosen (do not remove) the cap. This will keep the cooling system from becoming pressurized and the fluid should leak out slower. The engine may run slightly hotter; however, you should be able to drive a short distance at moderate speeds. Keep the radiator full of water and stop if the engine begins to overheat.

Expansion Tank

The expansion tank stores excess radiator fluid for the cooling system. As the temperature of the engine increases, the radiator fluid expands and some of it goes into the expansion tank. When the engine cools down, the fluid in the expansion tank is syphoned back into the radiator. This allows the cooling system to remain completely full at all times and helps prevent rust inside the radiator.

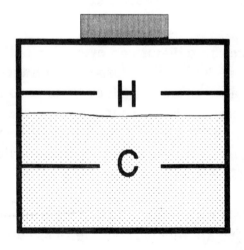

The expansion tank is convenient and safe. The fluid level in the transparent container can be quickly checked without removing the radiator cap. The HOT (H) level is correct when the engine is warm. The COLD (C) level is correct when the engine is cold. Do not overfill the expansion tank. The expansion tank is connected to the radiator with a small rubber hose.

Check the level of the radiator fluid in the expansion tank each WEEK. The fluid should be between the HOT (upper) and COLD (lower) marks. If the fluid level is low, add some clean water, to reach the COLD (lower) level. During cold weather, add anti-freeze.

If the fluid level is very low or the tank is empty, check for leaks in the radiator system. Driving without enough radiator fluid can cause the engine to overheat. If the small rubber hose between the expansion tank and radiator cap is leaking, replace it. Use new hose clamps.

Hoses & Hose Clamps

The engine and the radiator are connected by rubber hoses. These hoses are flexible and allow some movement as the car is driven. Hose clamps prevent leaks near the ends of the hoses. All cars have two large hoses connected to the radiator and two small hoses connected to the heater system. There may be several more smaller hoses on the engine. Hose clamps are on the both ends of each hose.

A leak in any one of the radiator hoses can cause the engine to overheat.

Check for leaks every 2 MONTHS. Look for leaks, cracks, or other damage to the hoses. If the hose is leaking near a clamp, tighten the clamp. Replace all the hoses and clamps every 4 YEARS. Always use new clamps with a new hose.

Radiator Fan

The radiator fan blows air through the radiator. This cools the radiator fluid and prevents the engine from overheating. The fan can be mechanical or electric.

Mechanical Fan

A belt turns the mechanical fan. Some mechanical fans are sensitive to heat. In other words, they can turn slower when the engine is cool and faster when the engine is hot. This reduces the amount of power needed to turn the fan and saves fuel.

A **heat sensitive** fan should rotate easily (without moving the belt) when the engine is OFF and COOL. When the engine is OFF and HOT (normal operating temperature), the fan should turn, but not as easily.

Another type of mechanical fan has plastic blades. These flexible blades change shape at various engine speeds to save fuel and provide adequate cooling for the radiator fluid.

If the mechanical fan is damaged, simply unbolt it from the water pump pulley and install a new one.

Electric Fan

An electric fan is turned by a small electric motor with power from the battery. It is fastened to the radiator and operates by a temperature switch. When the radiator fluid gets hot, the switch turns the fan ON. When the fluid cools down, the switch turns the fan OFF. The electric fan may be OFF while driving, because plenty of air is flowing through the radiator. Likewise, the fan may come ON anytime the fluid is hot.

If the electrical fan does not operate, check the fuse box. If the fuses are OK, Check the electrical connections at the fan and the temperature switch on the radiator. In emergency situations, you may be able to connect the fan directly to the battery causing it to run at all times. Note: the black wire is NEGative (ground) and the other wire (red) is POSitive. Have proper repairs done as soon as possible.

Water Pump

The water pump circulates the radiator fluid between the engine and the radiator. This allows the radiator fluid to absorb heat from the engine and release it to the outside air as it passes through the radiator. The water pump is located near the front of the engine and is turned by a belt. The lower radiator hose is connected to the water pump.

Always use a 50/50 mixture of water and coolant as radiator fluid. The coolant contains lubricants for the water pump and prevents rust in the cooling system. Maintain the proper tension on the belt. Replace the water pump every 4 YEARS.

The water pump must be removed to replace the timing belt on most engines. Therefore, consider replacing both items at the same time.

Thermostat

The thermostat adjusts the flow of the radiator fluid so the engine will warm up quickly and maintain the proper temperature under all driving conditions. Both cold  and very hot engine temperatures can cause poor engine performance, waste fuel, and damage the engine. The thermostat is normally located where the upper radiator hose attaches to the engine.

When the engine is cold, the thermostat closes to prevent the radiator fluid from going through the radiator. This allows the engine to warm up quickly (about 10 minutes). As the engine warms up to the normal operating temperature, the thermostat will open to allow the radiator fluid to circulate through the radiator and maintain the proper temperature.

Replace the thermostat every 4 YEARS. The thermostat will have a temperature (°C or °F) stamped on it. This is the temperature at which the thermostat begins to open as the water is heated (not the engine operating temperature). Do not drive without the thermostat. The engine may overheat or take longer to warm up.

If the thermostat does not open, the engine will overheat. If the thermostat stays open, the engine will take longer to reach the normal operating temperature.

Replacing the thermostat is not difficult. Wait until the engine cools down. Drain the radiator fluid from the radiator. Remove the upper radiator hose where it attaches to the engine. Remove the thermostat cover. Remove the old thermostat and gasket. Install a new thermostat and gasket (use gasket sealer, if necessary). Replace the cover and hose. Refill the radiator.

Heater

The heater uses hot radiator fluid to warm the air inside the car. The hot fluid flows from the engine through a radiator underneath the dashboard. An electric fan blows air through the radiator which warms the air. This warm air can be directed up towards the windshield or down towards your feet.

The rear window heater uses electric power from the battery to heat small wires attached to the window.

Heater Temperature Selector

The temperature selector controls a small valve and regulates the amount of radiator fluid which can flow through the heater radiator. This valve closes when the selector is on COLD and opens when the selector is moved to HOT.

Move the temperature selector to the HOT position for about 10 minutes each WEEK while the engine is running. This allows the radiator fluid to circulate and lubricate the heater system. If the heater controls do not move easily, lubricate them.

Move the heater temperature selector to **HOT** when changing the radiator fluid to remove the fluid in the heater system.

Air Conditioning

The air conditioner cools the air  inside the car by using a special compressed gas to "soak up" heat inside the car and release it to the outside air. When heat is removed from inside the car, it becomes cooler. The A/C system operates on a similar principal as the engine cooling system; however, the two systems are independent.

> The A/C requires power from the engine to operate and usually reduces the fuel economy of the car (lower MPG). While driving at highway speeds, however, using the A/C can actually save fuel as compared to driving with the windows open.

Using the A/C can cause the engine to overheat, especially when driving at slow speeds in very hot weather.

Compressor

The compressor is located near the front of the engine and is turned by a belt. The pulley attached to the compressor has a electric clutch which can be switched ON or OFF, depending on the needs of the A/C system.

Many cars have a button on the dashboard which can switch the A/C compressor **ON** or

Condenser

The condenser radiator is located in front of the engine radiator. This is where the heat from inside the car is released to the outside air.

Dryer

The dryer filters moister from the gas inside the A/C system. A sight glass may be available to visually check the condition of the gas inside the system.

Evaporator

The evaporator radiator is inside the car under the dashboard. This is where heat inside the car is absorbed by the expanding gas and produces the cooling effect. A small electric fan under the dashboard blows air through the evaporator radiator.

A/C Controls

The A/C controls are the hoses, electric wires, switches, and connectors which are necessary for proper A/C operation.

Turn the A/C OFF when extra power is needed from the engine, such as when starting the engine, going uphill, or passing another car. Switch the A/C OFF when the engine begins to overheat. Avoid switching the A/C OFF and ON quickly. After turning it OFF, wait 15 seconds before switching it back ON.

A/C Maintenance

Every WEEK (even in cold weather), run the engine and A/C for about 10 minutes. This circulates the pressurized gas and lubricates the system. If the A/C is not used for several months, the pressurized gas may leak out. Using the A/C in cold weather will help defrost the windows.

Have the A/C system serviced by a qualified technician every 2 YEARS. Add more gas to the system, if necessary.

The air-conditioning system operates under very high pressure and with dangerous gases and therefore any major repairs should be done by qualified technicians according to the shop manual. All leaks in the A/C system should be located and repaired. Leaks from A/C systems are a major cause of air pollution.

TRANSMISSIONS

Power produced in the engine goes through the transmission and the wheels to make the car move. The transmission allows the car to move at different speeds and to stop the car while the engine continues to run. Universal joints, or constant velocity joints, connect the drive shaft to the transmission and wheels.

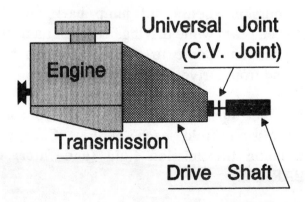

Automatic Transmission

The automatic transmission changes the
forward gears depending on the speed of
the car and the power being produced
by the engine. It uses a special
automatic transmission fluid to operate
both the clutch and transmission. The
filter inside the transmission cleans the
fluid as it circulates. A cooler may be
used to prevent the fluid from overheating.

```
P
R
N
D
2
1
```

If you use your car to pull a trailer or heavy
loads, install an automatic transmission cooler
to prevent the fluid from overheating.

After starting the engine, allow it to reach the idle
speed before shifting from Park (P) to Drive (D)
or Reverse (R). Move the fuel pedal gradually to
allow the transmission to shift easily. The
transmission should not jump back and forth
between gears while driving. This can damage the
transmission. Come to a complete stop before
shifting from Drive (D) to Reverse (R).

Use the dipstick to check the level of the
transmission fluid each WEEK. Change the
automatic transmission fluid (and filter) each
YEAR.

Dextron II and **Type F** are two different types of Automatic Transmission Fluid (ATF). Use the fluid recommended in the owners manual or shop manual. Do not mix different fluids.

Before checking the automatic transmission fluid level, drive the car until the engine warms up. Park in a level safe place and apply the parking brake. Leave the engine running. Slowly, shift the transmission level from Park (P) to First (1), then back to Park (P). Remove the A/T dipstick. Check the color of the fluid. Automatic transmission fluid is red or pink. If it is orange or brown, change it. Check the odor of the Fluid. If it smells burnt, change it. Wipe the dipstick clean. Replace it. Remove the dipstick again to check the fluid level. Add more clean fluid through the dipstick hole, if necessary, to maintain a FULL level. Do not overfill.

Dark or burnt smelling automatic transmission fluid indicates serious transmission damage.

Changing the automatic transmission fluid each year will help keep your car shifting smoothly. Always use a new gasket and change (or clean) the filter. Some cars use a replaceable paper filter, others use a metal screen, which can be cleaned and reused.

Manual Transmission

A manual transmission is basically a box with movable gears immersed in oil. The clutch is located between the transmission and engine. A fill plug located on the side of the transmission is 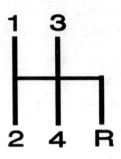 used to check the level of the oil. A drain plug is located near the bottom of the transmission.

> The manual transmission is less expensive and easier to repair as compared to the automatic transmission.

Stop your car before shifting between forward and reverse gears. The transmission lever may need to be pulled or pushed slightly in order to shift into reverse (R). Select the proper gear depending on the speed of the car. Avoid very fast or very slow engine speeds.

> Manual transmission normally requires a thick oil, such as SAE 90. Use the oil recommended in the owners manual or shop manual.

Remove the fill plug and check the oil level every 6 MONTHS. Change the oil each YEAR. If you drive through deep water, it is a good idea to check the fluid for water.

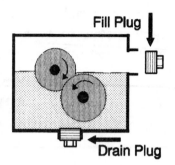

Fill Plug

Drain Plug

Overdrive

Overdrive is an extra gear installed on some transmissions to allow the engine to turn slower and use less

O / D

fuel when the car is cruising at highway speeds. Overdrive can be used on either manual or automatic transmissions.

Overdrive is usually the 5th gear on the manual transmission or the 4th gear (O) on the automatic transmission.

Use overdrive only when cruising at constant highway speeds. Maintain adequate engine speed by shifting down into a lower gear when going up steep hills or carrying heavy loads. Driving slow while using overdrive can damage the engine and transmission. Avoid using overdrive when pulling a heavy trailer or carrying heavy loads. Drive slower, but maintain higher engine speeds. The engine needs to turn faster and produce more power when pulling a heavy load.

> The engine speed (RPMs) should decrease when the transmission shifts into overdrive.

Clutch Pedal

The clutch pedal operates the clutch on the manual transmission. Pressing the pedal disengages the clutch (OFF) so the power from the engine cannot go to the wheels. Releasing the pedal engages the clutch (ON) allowing power from the engine to be transmitted through the transmission and to the wheels. The clutch pedal is connected to the clutch with either a hydraulic fluid system (similar to the brakes) or a wire cable.

> Do not leave your foot on the clutch pedal while driving the car (called riding-the-clutch).

Use your left foot to operate the clutch pedal. Keep your foot off of the clutch pedal as much as possible. When shifting gears, press the pedal, shift the transmission lever, and then release the pedal.

When the car stops, press the pedal, shift into Neutral (N), and then release the clutch pedal.

Test the clutch every 6 MONTHS. Press the pedal. It should feel firm, not spongy or soft. Shift into first gear. Release the clutch pedal slowly until the engine speed begins to decrease, then push the pedal back down. Note how far the pedal must move to make the engine speed start to decrease. It should move about two inches. Then shift into neutral. Release the pedal. Listen for strange sounds from the transmission. The transmission may make some noise, but any strange whirling or grinding sounds indicates trouble. Finally, press the pedal down slowly. The pedal should move about one inch before you feel some resistance.

If the clutch pedal feels spongy, air may be in the system. Bleed the air from the cylinder on the transmission. If the transmission makes strange noises, check the oil level in the transmission. If the clutch pedal moves more than two inches before the engine speed decreases or if there is less than one inch of play at the top position, it may need to be adjusted. If the clutch is worn out and cannot be adjusted, it must be replaced.

> When replacing the clutch, always install a new clutch release bearing.

Clutch Fluid Reservoir

The clutch fluid reservoir holds excess fluid for the hydraulic system. The upper mark on the fluid reservoir indicates the MAXimum fluid level and the lower mark indicates the MINimum fluid level. The reservoir is often  transparent to allow the fluid level to be seen easily without removing the cap. Do not drive the car when the fluid level is below the MINimum or lower mark. Use clean brake fluid in the clutch system.

If the car has a clutch pedal but no fluid reservoir, the clutch is operated by a cable.

Check the clutch fluid level each week. Add more clean brake fluid, as needed, to maintain the FULL level. Wipe off the top of the fluid reservoir before removing the cap to prevent dirt or water from getting into the reservoir. Replace the clutch fluid every 2 YEARS. Do not allow any dirt or water to fall into the clutch fluid reservoir when the cap is removed.

Drive Shaft & Universal Joints

The drive shaft transmits power from the engine to the wheels. Universal joints are the flexible connections, allowing the drive shaft to turn easily.

> A trans-axle is when the axle is connected directly to the transmission (front wheel drive). The universal joints are called Constant Velocity joints (C.V. joints).

Lubricate any grease fittings on the car, including the drive shaft and universal joints every 2 MONTHS. If these parts do not have any grease fittings, they are permanently lubricated; however, you may be able to install grease fitting.

> If you drive on sandy or dirt roads, cover the universal joints with small plastic bags to prevent sand/dirt from getting inside the parts.

Universal joints are bolted between the drive shaft and transmission (or differential). Simply support the drive shaft and unbolt these parts to remove them. C.V. Joints are more difficult to remove. For specific instructions, refer to the shop manual.

Differential

When the car is moving on a straight road, all the wheels are turning at the same speed. When the car turns a corners, the wheels on the outside travel further (and therefore slightly faster) than the wheels on the inside. The differential allows the wheels to turn at slightly different speeds. The differential is located between the two wheels and is connected to the axles. A 4WD car will have a differential for the rear wheels and another one for the front wheels.

Oil lubricates the moving parts inside the differential. Remove the fill plug, located on the side of the differential, to check the oil level and add more oil, as needed. The drain plug is located on the bottom. The drain plug may be magnetized to collect small pieces of metal from the oil.

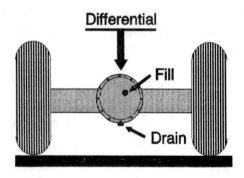

Limited-Slip Differential

A limited-slip differential allows at least some power to go to both wheels, even in slippery conditions. This improves traction and helps keep the car from becoming stuck. A locking differential transfers power evenly to both wheels which can be used in very slippery conditions.

> The limited-slip differential is good for any car. It should be required for a 4WD vehicle.

Differential Maintenance

Do not use different size tires on the same axle. This can damage the differential. Remove the fill plug to check the oil level every 6 MONTHS. Add more oil, when necessary. Do not overfill.

> The limited-slip differential may need a special lubricant. Use the oil recommended in the owners manual.

Remove the drain plug and change the oil every YEAR. After driving through deep water, check for water in the differential. If water is found in the oil, it should be changed. Dirt or water inside the differential will cause damage.

Speedometer & Odometer

The speedometer shows how fast the car is moving in Miles Per Hour (MPH), or Kilometer Per Hour (KPH), or both. The odometer shows how far the car has traveled in miles or kilometers. A flexible cable connects the speedometer to the transmission.

Sometimes the speedometer will start to vibrate, indicating that the cable is sticking. Lubricating the cable might help, but it may be easier just to replace the cable when it breaks.

Use the reset odometer to keep track of short trips or to help calculate MPG.

BRAKES

Brakes can be either disc or drum type. Disc brakes (front) use flat pads to push in against a flat disc. Drum brakes (rear) use curved pads to push out against a round drum. Parking brakes are attached to the rear brakes.

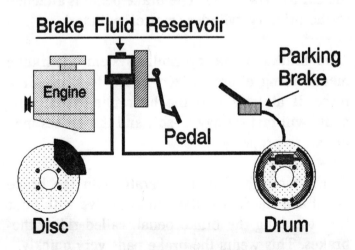

Extend the life of the brake pads by using the engine as a brake. Release the fuel pedal and allow the car to coast. Do not shift into neutral (N) or press the clutch pedal. The car will slow down gradually and the brakes can be used gently, as needed.

Do not slam-on-the-brakes. The car can be steered only when the front wheels are turning. Applying the brakes very hard can cause the wheels to lock-up and the car may slide out of control.

Brake Pedal

When you press the pedal the brake pads are pushed against the rotating wheels which causes the car to slow down. The brake pedal is attached to the primary cylinder (master cylinder).

The brakes use a hydraulic system. Hydraulic means using a pressurized liquid to transmit a force. If air gets into the hydraulic system, the pedal will feel spongy or soft and the brakes may not work properly.

Use your right foot to operate both the brake pedal and the fuel pedal. Do not drive with your foot touching the brake pedal, called riding-the-brakes. This wears the brake pads very quickly.

Test the brake pedal each time you start the engine. Do not drive when the brakes do not feel right or make unusual noise. Get them inspected to find out what the problem is.

After driving through deep water, test the brakes. When the brake pads get wet, they may not work very well. Press the pedal lightly while the car is moving in order to dry the pads.

Test The Brake Pedal

Press the brake pedal three times. The pedal should feel firm, not spongy or soft. Press the pedal hard and hold it down. It should not sink to the floor and you should be able to slide your left foot under the pedal.

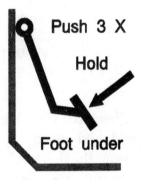

Push 3 X

Hold

Foot under

Brake Fluid Reservoir

The brake fluid reservoir holds fluid needed for the hydraulic system. The reservoir has two marks indicating the MAXimum and MINimum amounts of fluid. The brake fluid reservoir is located under the hood, directly in front of the drivers seat. It is attached to the top of the primary cylinder.

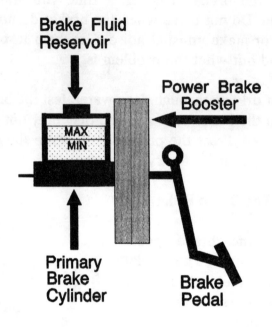

Brake Fluid Reservoir

Power Brake Booster

MAX
MIN

Primary Brake Cylinder

Brake Pedal

Check the fluid level in the reservoir each WEEK and add more clean brake fluid, as needed, to maintain the MAXimum level. A low fluid level can indicate a leak in the system.

Raise the hood to check the fluid level in the brake fluid reservoir. Add clean brake fluid, as needed, to maintain a MAXimum level. Most cars have transparent plastic reservoir so you can easily check the fluid level without removing the cap. If the reservoir is metal, remove the cap. Use caution not to allow dirt or water to get into the reservoir. This will damage the hydraulic system and cause leaks.

Do not drive a car when the level of fluid is
below the MINimum lever. The brakes may not
be able to stop the car.

Replace the brake fluid every 2 YEARS. Do not
keep open containers of brake fluid. It absorbs dirt
and water from the air. Brake fluid is very
corrosive and will damage paint.

All brake repairs must be done according to the
shop manual. After any brake repair, test the
brakes in a safe place at low speeds before driving
on the road.

Leaks in the hydraulic system usually occur at a
connection point. Locate the leak and tighten the
connection carefully. Do not damage the small
metal tubes or break the fittings. If the brake line
is damaged, replace it.

Bleeding Brakes

Bleeding the brakes means removing the air from
the hydraulic system in order to allow the brakes
to operate properly. A pressure-bleed, or power-
bleed, is quicker and more reliable than the two
person method described below, however, it
requires special tools.

If you want to bleed the brakes yourself, the following is a typical procedure. You will need a short length of clear rubber hose (1/4 inch ID), wrench, small container, and assistant to pump the pedal.

Check the brake fluid reservoir and add more brake fluid, if necessary, in order to reach the MAXimum level. Check the reservoir often while bleeding the brakes and do not allow the fluid level to drop below the MINimum mark.

Bleed one wheel at a time. Begin at the passenger side rear wheel, then the drivers-side rear wheel, then the passenger-side front wheel, and finally the drivers-side front wheel.

Locate the bleed screw on the wheel cylinder or caliper and attach the hose. The bleed screw is located on the inside of the wheel and looks like a grease fitting. It should be covered with a rubber cap.

Insert the other end of the hose into a small container. Have someone press the brake pedal and hold it down.

Open the bleed screw about 1/2 turn and allow the brake fluid to flow out of the bleed screw and into the jar. The brake pedal will slowly sink to the floor.

When the pedal touches the floor, tighten the bleed screw. Then release the pedal. Repeat, as needed, three times or more, if air bubbles are coming out of the bleed screw. Then do the next wheel.

Power Brakes

Power brakes use vacuum from the engine to reduce the amount of force needed to operate the brake pedal. This type of brake system has an additional part called the power brake booster. The booster is attached to the back of the primary brake cylinder. It looks like two large round pie pans fastened together. A large rubber hose connects the booster to the engine.

Check the hose connecting the power brake booster to the engine every 2 MONTHS to be sure it is not damaged or leaking. If this hose is leaking, the power brakes will not operate properly and unfiltered air can get inside the engine.

> If the power brakes malfunction for any reason, the brake pedal must be pushed very hard to stop the car.

It is easy to test the power brake system. When the car is parked and the engine OFF, press the brake pedal four times. The first time the pedal is pressed, it should feel normal. Then each time the pedal is pressed, it should feel harder.

Another way to test the power brake system is to press and hold the brake pedal down as you start the engine. The brake pedal should move down slightly.

Drum Brakes

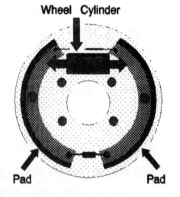

Wheel Cylinder

A drum brake pushes two curved brake pads (or shoes) outward on a rotating drum. Drum brakes are used on the rear wheels of the car because they provide a simple method of attaching the parking

Pad   Pad

brake system. Drum brakes tend to fade, or loose their ability to stop the car when they get hot.

The brakes should not make any unusual noise. If dragging or scrapping sounds are heard from the wheels, have the brakes inspected.

Avoid sudden stops and apply the brakes gently when moving in reverse. The drum brake pads are adjusted automatically when the car moves backwards and the brakes are applied. Sudden stops in reverse can damage the pads.

Inspect the brakes every 6 MONTHS. Adjust or replace the parts, as needed, according to the shop manual.

Excessive use of the brakes and sudden stops will cause the pads to wear out quickly.

Brake Inspection

Check the minimum thickness of the pads. Check for leaks near the wheel cylinders. Check the drum for scratches or cracks. Remove the tire and brake drum in order to inspect the pads, wheel cylinders, and drums. This is not difficult and many brake shops will preform this service free of charge. Refer to the shop manual for specific instructions.

Asbestos is used in some brake pads. Do not breath the dust near the brakes.

Both front brakes, or both rear brakes, must be repaired at the same time. Do not repair one wheel only. If any part of the brake pad is less than 1/16 inch thick (thickness of a nickel), replace all the pads on both wheels. Most new brake pads are glued to the metal shoe, however, if the pads are riveted to the metal shoes, the pad must be 1/16 inch above the rivets.

Brake Repairs

Old brake fluid can make the rubber seals leak. If any of the wheel cylinders is leaking, repair or replace all the cylinders. Replacing the cylinders is usually easier, but more expensive than repairing them. Most wheel cylinders, however, can be rebuilt easily with a few new parts. Install new clean brake fluid and bleed the system, too.

Do not press the brake pedal or operate the parking brake when the brake drum or caliper has been removed. This could allow the brakes to come apart or be damaged.

If the brake drum is scratched or cracked, it must be repaired or replaced. Turning the drum can remove small scratches. Large scratches or cracks in the drum should not be repaired; install a new drum. The inside diameter of both drums is the same. The maximum safe inside diameter can be found stamped on the drum.

Drum brakes should be adjusted when new pads are installed. Most drum brakes are automatically adjusted when you press the brake pedal while in reverse. Apply the brakes gently when backing up to prevent damage to the pads.

Replacing the pads is not difficult; however, this job should be done by a qualified person. Follow the directions in the shop manual and install pads recommended by the manufacturer.

Cheap pads will often make noise. If your old pads did not make noise, you certainly want new pads which are quiet as well. Get assurance from the mechanic that your pads are good quality.

Disc Brakes

A disc brake pushes two flat brake pads inward on a rotating brake disc, or rotor. Compared to the drum brake, the disc brake provides better performance and reliability. They are fade resistant. In other words, they maintain the ability to stop the car even during heavy use. Disc brakes work even in wet conditions and dry off quickly.

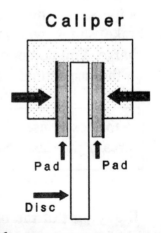

137

The disc brake pad is flat, wears evenly, and adjust automatically. Disc brakes are often used on the front wheels of the car. When the car stops, the weight of the car shifts forward. Therefore, the front brakes may be larger and wear out faster than the rear brakes.

> Avoid sudden stops. Excessive hard braking and sudden stops can wear the pads quickly.

Brake Inspection

Inspect the brakes every 6 MONTHS. Check the minimum thickness of the pads. Check for leaks near the calipers. Check the disc (rotor) for scratches or cracks.

Remove the tire in order to inspect the pads, calipers, and rotors. This is not difficult and many brake shops will preform this service free of charge. You do not need to remove the calipers to do the inspection.

> Asbestos is used in some brake pads. Do not breath the dust near the brakes.

If any part of the brake pad is less than 1/16 in (thickness of a nickel), replace all the pads on that axle. If the brake pads are riveted to the metal shoes, the pad must be 1/16 inch above the rivets. Both front brakes or both rear brakes must be repaired at the same time. Do not repair one wheel only.

Brake Repairs

Old brake fluid can make the rubber seals leak. If any of the calipers is leaking, repair or replace all the calipers. Replacing the calipers is usually easier, but more expensive than repairing them. Most calipers, however, can be rebuilt easily with a few new parts. Install new clean brake fluid and bleed the system, too.

If the brake disc (rotor) is scratched or cracked, it must be repaired or replaced. The disc can be turned to remove small scratches or cracks. Large scratches or cracks in the disc should not be repaired; install a new disc. If the discs are turned, be sure the thickness of the disc is above the minimum thickness found stamped on the disc.

Disc brakes automatically adjust the position of the pads each time the brakes are used. No other adjustment is normally required until the pads are replaced.

Replacing the pads is not difficult; however, this job should be done by a qualified person. Follow the directions in the shop manual and install pads recommended by the manufacturer.

Cheap pads will often make noise. If your old pads did not make noise, you certainly want new pads which are quiet as well. Get assurance from the mechanic that your pads are good quality.

Parking Brakes

Parking brakes, or hand brakes, are used to keep the car from rolling when it is parked. These brakes are not "emergency brakes"; they may not be able to stop a moving car. The parking brake lever is attached to the rear brakes with a cable.

Apply the parking brake firmly to reduce the chance of driving with the brake partially engaged.

Test the parking brakes every 6 MONTHS and adjust or repair them, as needed. An adjusting nut is located on the parking brake cable underneath the car. Tighten or loosen the nut, as required, to adjust the parking brakes. Do not over-tighten the parking brakes. This can cause unnecessary brake pad wear or the parking brakes may not work properly.

STEERING & SUSPENSION

The steering wheel controls the position of the front wheels, allowing you to turn the car. The tires and suspension let the wheels to move up and down to provide a smooth ride on bumpy roads. Each wheel will have some combination of shock absorber and spring.

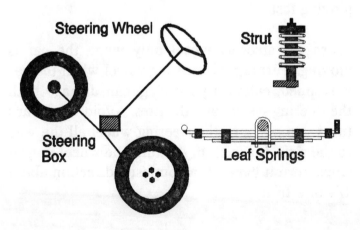

Steering Wheel

Strut

Steering Box

Leaf Springs

Fast driving and over-loading the car can damage the steering or suspension.

Steering Wheel

The steering wheel controls the position of the front wheels. It is attached to a long tube, called the steering column which should collapse in case of an accident to prevent serious injuries to the driver. After any accident, or when the steering wheel feels loose, have it inspected by a qualified repair shop.

Keep both hands on the steering wheel while driving the car and use a hand-over-hand method to turn the wheel. Turn the steering wheel slowly. Avoid sudden turns, especially when the car is moving fast.

Turn the steering wheel only when the car is moving. Turning the steering wheel when the car is stopped, called dry-steering, can damage both the steering system and the tires. Avoid very sharp turns. Do not turn the steering wheel all the way to the right (or left). If you turn the wheel until it stops, turn it back in the opposite direction about 1/4 of a turn.

Adjust The Steering Wheel

Many newer cars have an adjustable steering wheel which can be moved up or down, depending on the position which is most comfortable you. The adjustment lever is usually on the steering column. Adjust it before starting the engine.

Do not adjust the steering wheel while the car is moving.

Test The Steering Wheel

The distance the steering wheel must be turned to cause the front wheels to move is called "play" or looseness. In theory, there should be no play in the steering system and any slight movement of the steering wheel would produce some movement of the front tires. However, the steering system must be flexible to allow the front wheels to move both up-and-down and right-and-left as the car is driven.

Put the key switch in the ON position. Do not start the engine. Hold the top of the steering wheel with your right hand, while at the same time looking out at the left front tire. Turn the steering wheel very slowly to the left until the tire starts to move to the left. Stop. (Do not dry-steer).

Turn the steering wheel back slowly to the right until the tire starts to move to the right. Stop. Repeat steps 3 and 4, measuring the approximate distance your right hand is moving.

Normal play for most steering wheels is about one inch. If the play is more than 2 inches, the steering system should be inspected and repaired.

Steering Box

The steering box changes the circular movement of the steering wheel into a back-and-forth motion needed to make the tires move to the left or right. The steering box is connected to the bottom of the steering column. Tie rods connect the steering box to the front wheels.

Add grease to any grease fittings on the steering box every 2 MONTHS. Check the oil level in the steering box every 6 MONTHS. Add more oil when necessary. Note: If the car has power steering, the power steering fluid circulates through the steering box and there is no oil. Refer to the next section for more information.

Power Steering

Power steering (P/S) allows the steering wheel to be turned with less effort. The engine actually supplies the "power" to turn the power steering pump. This pump forces a special fluid through the steering box to reduce the effort needed to turn the steering wheel. The power steering fluid reservoir holds a supply of fluid needed for the system. Both the P/S pump and fluid reservoir are located near the engine. The pump is turned by a belt.

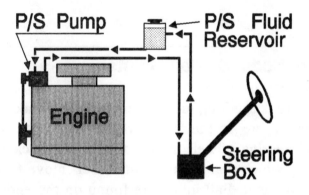

Check the P/S fluid level each WEEK. Add more clean P/S fluid, as needed. Do not overfill. A low P/S fluid level can cause a whining sound and the steering wheel may be harder to turn. Check for leaks.

If the power steering system should fail, greater effort will be required to steer the car.

Change the P/S fluid every 2 YEARS. Most P/S systems use Auto Transmission Fluid (ATF). Some cars require a special fluid. Use the fluid recommended in the owners manual. If you drive without adequate fluid or the wrong type of fluid in the system, the P/S pump will be damaged.

The P/S reservoir may have a small dipstick attached to the cap or the reservoir may have marks indicating the MAXimum and MINimum fluid levels. Do not overfill. Do not allow dirt or water to get into the P/S fluid reservoir. Wipe off the top of the reservoir before removing the cap.

Tie Rods & Ball Joints

Tie rods are long metal tubes which connect the steering box to the front wheels. When you turn the steering wheel, the tie rods move back and forth which makes the front wheels move to the left or right. Ball joints are found on the ends of the tie rods and provide some flexibility to the steering system. Flexibility is needed as the wheels move up and down on bumpy roads.

Ball-joints are available in both left-side and right-side parts. They may look identical, but they have different threads. **LH = Left Hand** and **RH = Right Hand**.

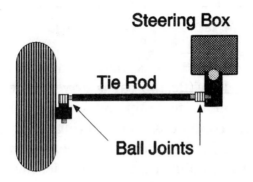

Steering Box

Tie Rod

Ball Joints

If the ball joints have grease fittings, lubricate them every 2 MONTHS. There may also be other grease fittings on the car which need lubrication. Newer cars have fewer grease fittings. The ball joints may be permanently lubricated.

Test The Tie Rod

Grab the tie rod firmly. Shake it and twist it. The tie rod may move a little, however, it should not be loose. If it is loose, the ball joints should be checked and replaced, if necessary.

After replacing a tie rod or ball joint, the alignment of the wheels may need to be checked. Adjustments to the wheels alignment are made by turning the tie rods. Turning the tie rod one way increases the distance between the wheels, turning the opposite direction decreases the distance. Refer to the section in this chapter about wheel alignment.

Shock Absorbers & Springs

The shock absorbers and springs provide a smooth ride while the car is driven. The wheels must be able to move up and down depending on the road conditions. The springs support the weight, while the shock absorbers prevent the springs from bouncing too much (ie. they absorb the shocks). The total weight of the car, the speed the car is driven, and the road conditions will also determine the smoothness of the ride.

A shock absorber is located near each wheel. They move in and out as the wheels move up and down. The most common type are filled with oil. Special shocks may be filled with a compressed gas. Another small shock absorber, called a steering damper, may be connected to the steering system to reduce vibrations in the steering wheel.

Firm or Soft

Firm (heavy duty) shock absorbers and springs will provide a better ride for heavier cars on rough roads; however, they may produce a bouncy ride under normal driving conditions. Soft shock absorbers and springs will produce a smooth ride for lighter loads on improved roads; however, they may allow the car to bottom-out with heavier loads on rough roads. Adjustable shock absorbers/springs are available which can be adjusted with compressed air for different loads and road conditions.

> For the smoothest ride, use the softest shock absorbers and springs combination that does not allow the car to bottom-out.

Do not increase the speed of the car on rough roads, even though the car seems to ride smoother at faster speeds. This can damage the suspension system.

Shock Absorber & Spring Maintenance

Do not overload the car. Do not drive fast on bumpy roads. Test the shock absorbers and springs every 6 MONTHS. Replace the shock absorbers, springs, or struts as needed.

Coil Springs

Coil springs are typical springs, just very big. These round springs are made from metal rods about 1/2 inch in diameter. The top of the spring is connected to the frame of the car and the bottom is connected near the wheel.

Leaf Springs

Leaf springs are flat pieces of metal. The longer pieces are on top and the shorter pieces are near the bottom. Both ends of the leaf spring are attached to the frame of the car and the center of the spring is attached near the wheel. This type of spring is usually the easiest to replace.

Torsion Bar

A torsion bar spring is a long metal rod which acts like a spring when it is twisted. One end of the bar is fastened to the car frame and the other end of the bar is attached near the wheel. Torsion bars are most commonly used on the front wheels and are attached to the frame of the car near the rear axle.

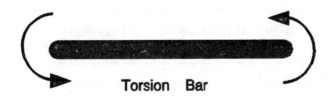

Torsion Bar

Struts

Struts are a special type of suspension found on many new cars. The shock absorber is inside the coil spring. The wheel alignment should be checked after replacing the struts. With good driving habits, the springs should never need to be replaced.

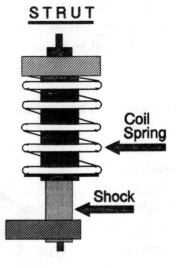

STRUT

Coil Spring

Shock

As the shock absorbers wear out, the car will begin to bounce more and may be hard to control while turning and stopping.

Test The Springs & Shocks

Push down on one corner on the car, then let go quickly. The car should bounce up, down, and then stop on the way up. If the car continues to bounce up and down, replace the shocks. Repeat this test for all four shocks, if necessary.

The car should sit level. A car with a broken spring or damaged suspension will not sit level.

Look underneath the car. Check the springs for cracks or damage. A broken or loose spring usually makes noise while the car is driven.

Replacing The Springs & Shocks

Replacing a standard shock absorber is very easy and can improve the handling of the car. Most shocks are simply bolted in place. New rubber bushings should come with each shock absorber, if not, purchase these parts separately. Be sure you have the right type of shock absorber and follow the directions given in the shop manual.

Do not attempt to replace a strut. The coil spring may need to be compressed tightly to remove the old strut or install the new one and the wheel alignment may need to be adjusted.

Replace the shocks or springs in pairs, even if only one is damaged. For example, change the front two shock absorbers at the same time.

The weight of the car must be supported using a jack stand when replacing the springs. Sometimes the spring must be compressed to remove and replace them without injury or car damage (special tools are available).

Rubber Bushings

Rubber bushings are used to absorb vibrations on many car parts. The shock absorbers, springs, radiators, engine (motor mounts), transmission, car body, tie rods, and exhaust parts may all have several bushings. Check the bushings every 6 MONTHS. Replace them, as needed, according to the shop manual.

Dirt and water on the bushings should not cause damage. Heat, sunlight, fuel, oil, brake fluid, and old age can damage the bushings. A broken or loose bushing will cause parts to vibrate and rattle. This can damage the more expensive parts of the car. Replacing bushings is easier and less expensive than repairing the more expensive car parts.

Test The Bushings

Locate the bushing(s). Inspect the bushings one at a time. Wipe the dirt off and look for cracks in the rubber. If it is broken or loose, replace it.

Touch the rubber bushing. It should be soft, but firm. If it is very soft or very hard, replace it. Try moving the part connected to the rubber bushing. It may move a little, but it should not be loose. If it is loose, replace it. A loose bushing can sometimes be tightened by adjusting the part connected to the bushings. Do not over-tighten. Replace a broken or old bushing.

Wheel Bearings

Each wheel turns on two sets of bearings: the inner bearing and outer bearing. These bearings allow the wheels to turn easily and improve the fuel economy (higher MPG) and handling ability of the car. Most bearing are lubricated with grease; however, some use the differential oil. The wheel may have grease fittings for the bearings or the bearing may need to be removed to add more grease. Newer cars may have permanently lubricated wheel bearings which do not need additional grease.

Check the wheel bearings every 6 MONTHS, or after driving through deep water. Do not overload the car or drive fast on rough roads. Adjust, lubricate, or replace the wheel bearings, as needed, according to the shop manual.

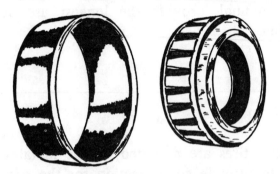

Wheel bearings are relatively inexpensive parts and can usually be easily replaced. If the bearings are not adjusted or lubricated properly, more serious (and expensive) wheel damage may occur.

If the bearing is too tight, it cannot turn easily and may get very hot and burn up. If the bearing is too loose, it will wobble and break.

Test The Bearings

Jack one of the wheels slightly off the ground. Hold the wheel at the top and bottom. Shake it. A little movement is normal, but the wheel should not be loose. Hold the wheel on the right and left. Shake it. Spin the wheel forward and backwards while listening for grinding sounds. If the wheel is loose or makes strange sounds, inspect the bearings. Test all four wheels.

155

Bearings should be tightened until they begin to drag or bind, then loosen them just slightly so they spin freely. Proper adjustments, according to the shop manual, provide the longest use of the bearing.

Tires

Rubber tires are mounted on the metal wheel rims to provide good traction for the car. The most important dimensions of a tire are the inside diameter (ID) and width (W). A P185/70R13 tire is 185mm wide and 13 inches in diameter. All tires should be the same size. Using different size tires can damage both the tires and the transmission. Drive slow (less than 45 MPH) when using the compact spare tire.

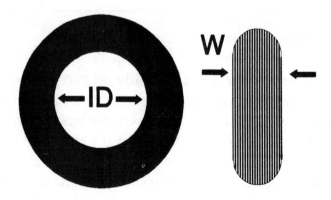

Tires are rated on a standard system. **Temperature** and **Traction** can be rated A, B, or C (A=Best) and **Treadwear** 100 (standard). The best tires will have a Temperature rating of A.

Wear-Bars

Tire tread refers to the depth of the small grooves on the outside of the tires. If a tire does not have enough tread, the car may not be able to stop quickly or can slide out-of-control. Wear-bars are small strips of rubber made into the tire which indicated the minimum safe tire tread (see illustration).

To avoid 90% of all tire problems, replace the tires when the wear-bars show across the tire tread or when the tread is about 1/16 inch deep.

Tire Maintenance

Before driving the car, check for a flat tire. Avoid fast starts and sudden stops. Do not allow the tires to spin or slide on the road. Check the air pressure and tread on each tire (including the spare) each WEEK. Use an accurate pressure gauge and inflate to the recommended pressure. Do not over-inflate. Balance and rotate the tires every 6 MONTHS.

Keep caps on the tire stems (where air is added). Dirt or water can damage the valve and cause a slow leak. If the tire stem is short, install tire stem extenders.

Driving the car with under-inflated tires can damage the tire and cause low fuel economy (low MPG). Overinflated tires can suddenly burst while driving. Always maintain proper tire pressure and do not overload the car.

Some road surfaces can cause the tires to make a strange noise. Small rocks in the tire tread or hubcaps can cause clicking sounds while driving.

Tire Wear Patterns Can Indicate Problem

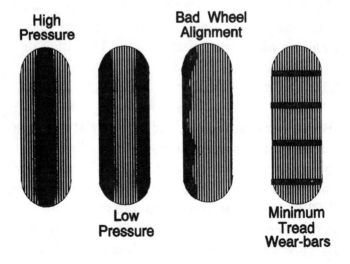

High Pressure

Bad Wheel Alignment

Low Pressure

Minimum Tread Wear-bars

Test The Tires

Check the tire pressure with an accurate tire pressure gauge when the tire is cold (before the car has been driven very far). Driving the car will cause the tire pressure to increase slightly. If the tire pressure was correct when the tire was cold, do not release any air from the tire.

Check the tire tread. It should be the same across the tire. If the tread is wearing more in the center of the tire, it may be overinflated. If the tread is wearing more on the outside of the tire, it may not have enough air. Strange tread wear patterns may be caused by poor wheel alignment or a defective tire.

Bad tires can cause some steering and handling problems. If the tire wobbles or the car pulls to one side, rotate the tires. If the problem persist, check the wheel-axle assembly. If the problem moves with the tire, check the tires.

Tubeless Tires

Early cars had a rubber tube (innertube) inside the tire to hold the air. Today, most tires are tubeless and do not have innertubes. Tubeless tires actually bond against the metal wheel rim to hold the air pressure. These tires require special tools and training to be mounted properly.

Tire Repairs

A slow leak in the tire is often near the tire valve (inside the tire stem). Put a little bit of water inside the valve stem and watch for small bubbles. Tighten the valve (screw it in) or replace it and then inflate the tire to the correct pressure. Install protective caps on all the valve stems. Small cans of compressed air and sealer are available at many auto parts stores which can be used to stop a small leak and inflate the tire.

Although most cars today use tubeless tires, innertubes can be repaired with patches. These patches can be either cold or hot. Cold patches are the easiest to use, but may not last very long. Hot patches are the preferred method because the heat allows the glue to bond with the rubber tube.

Balancing & Rotating Tires

Tires need to be properly balanced to avoid wobbling at high speeds (over 30 MPH). Small weights are attached to the wheel rims, as needed. Rotate the tires from the front to the back every 6 MONTHS, or as recommended.

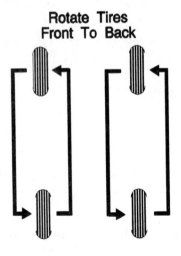

Rotate Tires
Front To Back

When you buy new tires, ask for free tire rotation and balancing every 6 MONTHS (6000 miles). Some tire stores include this service in the purchase price.

Wheel Alignment

Wheel alignment, or the exact position of each wheel, is extremely important for safe handling of the car and long tire life. These adjustments must be made by a qualified mechanic with the proper specifications from the shop manual and special equipment.

Drive slowly over bumps and on bumpy roads. Check the wheel alignment every 2 YEARS, or after any accident. Improper wheel alignment will cause unnecessary tire wear, difficult handling, and reduced fuel economy.

If you hit a bump while driving, slow down and try to have the wheels straight ahead. Hitting a bump while turning can damage the alignment.

Test Wheel Alignment

Drive the car on a smooth level road. The steering wheel should not pull to either side.

> Problems with the brakes or low tire pressure can also cause the steering wheel to pull to one side. Check the brakes and tire pressure before investing in a wheel alignment.

Front wheel drive cars with four wheel independent suspension systems need all four wheels aligned. Rear wheel drive cars usually need only the front two wheels aligned.

There are several adjustments necessary for proper wheel alignment: toe-in, toe-out, caster, and camber. All of these adjustment must be made according to the shop manual using very precise measurements. Find an experienced and patient technician for accurate adjustments.

There are "lifetime alignment" offers at some tire stores. Of course, if you have a new car and you want to keep it for a long time, this may be a good investment. If you car is older or you plan to trade it soon, just pay for individual alignments, as needed.

SAFETY ITEMS

The lights, horn, seat belts, windshield wipers, and car body are just some of the safety items found on your car. These and other safety items provided for your safety and the safety of others. Always use safety items properly and never disconnect or bypass them.

Although all cars must have an annual safety inspection before being allowed onto the highways, the inspection is not always enforced properly. Check you car regularly to be sure it is in safe driving condition.

> Safety items can help to prevent accidents and reduce harmful pollution.

Lights

Every car should have a working system of lights. Brake lights are needed to warn other cars that you are slowing down or stopping. Headlights are needed at night both to improve your visibility and to allow other drivers to see your car. Other lights, such as turn signals, emergency flashers, and interior lights are important safety items, too.

> When driving in fog, use the headlights on **LOW**. The high beam will cause more light to be reflected in the fog and can limit your visibility.

Whenever your visibility is limited by darkness, fog, or bad weather, drive slower and be ready to stop quickly. Watch for other cars which may have pulled off of the road to stop. If you stop on the side of the road, use the emergency flashers, turn signals, or road flares to warn other drivers.

Adjusting Lights

Headlights can be adjusted up/down or right/left by turning the adjusting screws located near the headlights. If the headlights are out of adjustment or shinning too high, they may blind other drivers and cause an accident. The drivers-side headlight should shine almost straight ahead. The other headlight should shine slightly to the right (or outside).

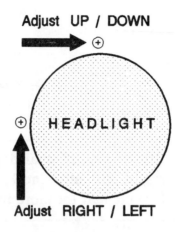

Adjust UP / DOWN

HEADLIGHT

Adjust RIGHT / LEFT

Check each of the lights to be sure they are operating correctly each WEEK. Wash the lights. A layer of dust can reduce their brightness.

Driving without proper lights can be very dangerous. You may not be able to see the road at night or other drivers may not be warned that your car is stopping or turning. These situations could result in an accident.

Repairing Lights

Check for a broken fuse. Check for a broken bulb. Clean and tighten loose electrical connections. The following illustrations demonstrate how to change bulbs.

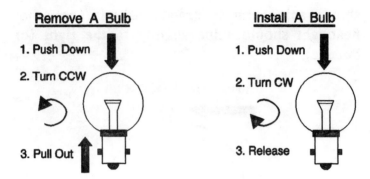

The most difficult part of changing the bulb may be getting to the bulb. Check the owners manual or shop manual for more information.

Horn

The horn should be used to warn other drivers or pedestrians. A friendly beep-beep should not be considered rude; however, a long "beeeeeeeeeep" can upset some people.

When driving behind another car, use extra caution when people are walking near the road. The pedestrian may step out of the way for the first car; but, if they do not expect another car, they might quickly step back into the road.

The horn button is located near the steering wheel. A common place for the horn button is the center of the steering wheel; however, many newer cars use several small buttons. Some cars have a horn operated by squeezing the outside of the steering wheel or by pushing the turn signal lever. Locate the horn button when driving a car for the first time.

Test the horn each WEEK. Do not wait until an emergency situation arises to start looking for the horn button or to find out that the horn is broken.

If the horn does not work, check the fuse box for a broken fuse. Check the wire connections at the horn. If the horn will not stop blowing, remove the wires from the horn (under the hood) or remove the horn fuse (in the fuse box).

Seat Belts

The seat belt is designed to protect the passenger in case of a serious accident; however, only seat belts which are worn properly can help prevent injuries. Both lap belts and shoulder harnesses are needed to prevent serious injuries. All adult passengers should wear seat belts and children should sit in a car seat.

Seat belts should be worn snug. If the seat belt is loose, it cannot provide adequate protection in case of an accident. If the seat belt is tight, it may be uncomfortable.

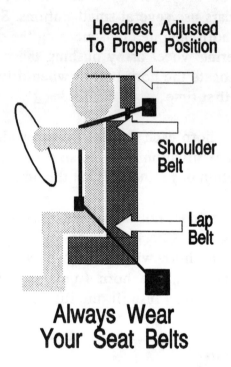

**Headrest Adjusted
To Proper Position**

**Shoulder
Belt**

**Lap
Belt**

Always Wear
Your Seat Belts

Do not worry about being trapped inside a wrecked car because of the seat belt. Passengers wearing seat belts receive fewer injuries.

Inspect the seat belt connections and be sure they are in good condition every 2 MONTHS. After any ACCIDENT: Inspect the seat belts carefully to be sure they were not damaged. Do not attempt to repair the seat belts. Damaged seat belts should always be replaced.

Safety Starting Switches

Safety starting switches prevent the engine from starting whenever there is an unsafe condition. Newer cars are more likely to have these switches.

1. **Transmission switch:** Shift the transmission lever to **P (Park)** or **N (Neutral)**.

2. **Seat belt switches:** Fasten the seat belts.

3. **Clutch switch:** Depress the clutch pedal.

4. **Brake switch:** Press and hold the brake pedal. Apply the parking brake.

If the safety starting switch does not work properly, the engine may not start at all or it could start in an unsafe condition.

The engine should start easily when all the starting switches are set properly. The engine will not make any sound and the headlights will not dim if a safety starting switch is not properly set. Refer to the shop manual for the exact location of the switches. Do not remove or adjust the safety starting switch to allow the engine to start when there is an unsafe condition.

Windshield Wipers

Windshield
Washer Fluid

The windshield wipers are used to wipe away rain or clean the windshield. It is very important that the rubber blades be in good condition to operate properly and avoid damage to the windshield. Some wipers have a built in a delay feature, allowing the wipers to operate once every few seconds when driving in a light rain or mist. A wiper may be on the rear window, too.

The wiper system should be able to spray water onto the windshield to help clean the windshield and allow the wipers to slide easily.

> Special washer fluid is available which helps prevent the windshield water from freezing in cold weather and remove stubborn dirt.

Do not operate the windshield wipers when the windshield is dry. Check the windshield washer reservoir and add water or cleaner, as needed, each WEEK. Replace the rubber wipers every 2 YEARS.

The wiper blades can be pulled away from the windshield to allow the inserts to be removed. Follow the directions provided with the inserts or have someone show you how to replace them. There are many different methods used to fasten the inserts to the wiper blade; however, most can be done quickly without special tools. Replacing only the rubber part of the wiper, called the insert, may be less expensive than replacing the entire blade.

In an emergency situation use sandpaper to remove some of the brittle rubber parts of the wiper which may allow the wipers to operate better for a little while. Replace the wipers as soon as possible.

Emission Controls

Emission controls help reduce the amount of air pollution. Newer cars will normally have more emission controls. Gasoline engines will have more emissions controls than a diesel engine.

Positive Crankcase Ventilation Valve

A PCV valve is on most gasoline engines. The valve removes harmful vapors from inside the engine and allows them to be burned with the fuel-air mixture. This increases fuel economy, reduces air pollution, and helps prevent contamination of the engine oil.

Exhaust Gas Recirculating Valve

The EGR valve allows some of the exhaust gases to be re-burned inside the engine which reduces harmful emissions. If the EGR valve is broken, the engine may backfire.

Catalytic Converter

A catalytic converter is part of the exhaust system and absorbs harmful gases before they are released at the rear of the car. Always use unleaded fuel to avoid damage to the expensive catalytic converter.

Do not park the car in tall grass or over any combustible material. The catalytic converter gets very **HOT** and could start a fire.

Air Pump

The air pump (compressor) injects compressed air into the hot exhaust gases in order to finish burning any unburned or partially burned fuel. The extra oxygen turns any poisonous CO into harmless CO_2.

The air pump can make a strange noise that might be confused with engine trouble.

Emission Control Maintenance

Use only the correct type of fuel to avoid damage to the emission controls. Inspect the hoses every 2 MONTHS. Replace the PCV valve and filter and have all the emission controls checked according to the shop manual every YEAR.

A clogged PCV valve can cause the engine to run rough and leak oil. Leaded gasoline can damage the catalytic converter and possibly clog the exhaust system. The engine may not start.

Removing the emission controls will not necessarily improve the fuel economy or performance of the engine. It can cause serious engine damage.

Removing the catalytic converter may allow the engine to run on regular gasoline and save a few dollars in fuel cost; however, it will cause unnecessary air pollution and shorten the life of the engine.

Diesel engines have very little, if any, pollution controls. Older cars had fewer and simpler items, compared with the newer gasoline engines. Also, older cars have lower pollution standards. So if you want to avoid dealing with pollution controls, buy a diesel engine or an older car.

Car Body

The car body protects the passengers while at the same time provides a basic shell to hold all the parts

of the car together. In case of an accident the car body is designed to be crushed and absorb the impact of the accident, thereby reducing the force felt by the passengers. This will, however, mean more damage to the car.

Washing The Car

Do not wash the car in the hot sun. Find a shady spot or wash it late in the day. Rinse the entire car with clean water before starting. Wash the top of the car first and work your way down, leaving the dirtiest sections for last. Do not scratch or rub stubborn dirty spots. Soak these spots with a wet rag for several minutes. Use mild soaps or dish-washing liquid when washing the car. Use a vinyl-plastic-rubber cleaner on these type of parts. It cleans the parts and keeps them from cracking.

Wash the car before waxing. Liquid waxes are easier to use, but may not last as long. Hard waxes require more rubbing and buffing, but will last longer.

Car Body Maintenance

Clean the car (inside and outside) each WEEK. Wax the car every 6 MONTHS.

> New polymer wax compounds actually bond to the cars paint and should last longer; however, they may be very expensive and need a professional application.

Removing Scratches

Use a rubbing compound to remove dull oxidized paint or small scratches. The rubbing compound actually removes a thin layer of paint, so do not use it too often. Follow the directions provided with the rubbing compound. Do not use rubbing compound or any abrasive cleaner on cars with clear protective coatings. If you are not sure, check with the dealership.

Repairing A Dent

Straighten the dented area as best as possible, using a hammer or a dent-puller tool. Try using a large suction cup (plumber's tool) to pull the dent out. Use sandpaper to remove any rust, dirt, and paint from the area. Use a fiberglass or putty filler to fill the hole. Let it dry completely. Smooth the area. Use a rasp and coarse sandpaper to achieve the approximate shape desired. Finish with smooth sandpaper (#200) and very smooth wet sandpaper (#400). Repaint the section of the car. Use a rust protection primer followed by several thin coats of car paint. Allow each coat to dry before adding the next. Fillers, sandpaper, and automotive paints are available at most auto parts stores.

Any large dent which may have damaged the steering, suspension, or car frame should be inspected by a qualified repair shop.

12

GOOD DRIVING HABITS

Most accidents can be avoided by maintaining both the speed and direction of the car within safe limits. However, good driving habits involve more than just pressing the gas pedal and turning the steering wheel. Good driving habits reduce the chances of being involved in an accident and extend the life of your car. If you want your car to last a long time follow these easy rules to safe driving. The most important safety feature in any car is a smart driver.

Accidents happen, but many accidents can be and should be avoided. If your car is not in good driving condition, have it repaired and do not risk being involved in an accident.

Patience

Patience is a good driving habit for every driver. People in a hurry tend to overlook safe driving habits and therefore, cause accidents. Are you in a hurry to have an accident or get a speeding ticket? Make two trips, instead of over-loading the car. Take a few minutes to check the car before each trip. Allow extra distance in front of your car in case you must stop quickly. Let the "tailgaters" pass.

Slow down. Enjoy life a little more and have more life to enjoy.

Loading The Car

Both the total weight in the car and the location of the weight are important. Although the owners manual gives specific weight and balance information for each car, no one actually measures each package or passenger.

Overloading the car can damage the springs, suspension, steering or tires. The car will also take much longer to stop and may go out of control while turning. When you must carry heavy items in the car, drive slower and use lower gears to maintain higher engine speeds.

Heavy Items

Heavy items should be put on the bottom and near the center of the car. This keeps the car from becoming top-heavy and allows the weight to be shared equally between all wheels. Otherwise, the car may be hard to control, especially when turning or stopping.

Light Items

Lighter bulky items can be carried on top of the car, if necessary. If the car becomes top-heavy with too much weight on the top, it can turn over or go out-of-control.

Remove Unnecessary Heavy Items

Unnecessary weight carried in the car wastes fuel and puts additional strain on the car. This can shorten the life of the car. Remove heavy items from the car, when they are not needed.

Tie Everything Down

Use rope or rubber tie-downs to hold everything in place. This prevents the items from rolling around causing personal injuries or car damage. A heavy item which is not tied down can cause the car to go out-of-control at high speeds. Even small items can cause serious injuries when the car stops suddenly.

Everyone should wear a seat belt whenever the car is moving. The seat belt can save your life.

Overloaded Car

Look at the tires. An overloaded car will appear to have flat tires, even when the tire pressure is correct. Make sure the tires are properly inflated, but do not overinflate them. Overloaded or overinflated tires can burst suddenly while driving, causing an accident.

Look at the springs and shock absorbers. If they are almost fully compressed, the car is overloaded. Each corner of the car should have some bounce and the axles should not hit the frame of the car. Overloading the car can damage the suspension system and cause an accident.

Carrying Heavy Loads

Drive slower to avoid damage to the transmission and suspension systems. Use extra caution going over bumps or driving on rough roads. Drive slow, but maintain adequate engine speed. Higher engine speed (RPMs) is needed to provide extra power.

If your car does not have a tachometer to indicate the engine speed (RPMs), turn the radio OFF and listen to the engine.

The Pre-Drive Inspection

Take a few minutes before you get into your car to be sure it is safe to leave. Walk around the car and look at the tires. Look for objects underneath or near the car. Look for leaks under the car. If you see a leak, locate the leak and check fluid level before starting the engine.

Before Starting The Engine

Check for loose objects in the car. Set the parking brake. Adjust the seat and headrest. Adjust the steering wheel. Fasten the seat belts. Adjust the mirrors. Check the pedals. Turn the key switch to ON and check the warning lights.

> The outside mirrors (left and right) should be adjusted to see the blind spots near the rear wheels.

After Starting The Engine

Did the engine start easily? Check the oil pressure indicator. Check the electrical system indicator. Check the fuel gauge. Check the brake pedal. Check the steering wheel. Check the horn. Clean the windshield. Release the parking brake. Be sure to check both mirrors before backing up.

> Do not "rev" the engine as soon as it starts. Avoid high engine speeds for several minutes.

While Driving

The transmission should shift smoothly. The car should stop easily when you press the brake pedal. Listen for any strange noises which might indicate a problem.

Although this may seem like a long list of things to do, the entire list should only take about two minutes. If there is a problem with the car, you can often avoid a road-side breakdown by determining the problem early.

Look, Listen, Feel, and Smell

Look where the car is going, but also look for other traffic and pedestrians and watch the gauges and warning lights on the dashboard. Listen for unusual sounds from the car. Feel the movements of the car and note any unusual vibrations. Smell any unusual odors.

> If you notice a problem with the car, stop the car before serious car damage results.

Scanning

Scanning is when you keep your eyes moving and avoid staring at one object for more than a few seconds. Think about what you are seeing and anticipate problems. Do not day-dream or drive on "auto-pilot".

> Stay at least **two seconds** behind the car in front of you. At night or during bad weather, stay back even longer and allow adequate stopping distance.

Slow and Steady

Speed up slowly and avoid jack-rabbit starts. Move along with the traffic while staying within the speed limit and driving according to the road conditions. Both very fast drivers and very slow drivers can cause accidents. Slow down gradually, using the engine as a brake, and avoid sudden stops. Fast starts and sudden stops waste fuel and wears out the brake pads.

> Slow down, unless there is a real emergency involving the possible loss of life. This helps avoid an accident, saves fuel, and can extend the life of your car.

After A Long Trip

After driving for a long time at highway speeds, allow the engine to idle for about 30 seconds before turning the key switch to OFF. If you were using the air conditioner, turn it OFF. This stabilizes the engine systems and prevents dieseling in gasoline engines.

"Dieseling" is when the engine continues to run (very slowly) after you turn it OFF. This can damage the engine and waste fuel.

> Do not press the fuel pedal and "rev" the engine while turning the key switch to OFF. This can damage the engine and cause dieseling.

OFF-ROAD DRIVING

Normal driving conditions assume the road is smooth, dry, and hard. When the road is bumpy, wet, or soft, off-road driving skills are needed to avoid becoming stuck or damaging the car. Off-road conditions can appear almost anywhere.

Use 4 Wheel Drive (4WD) only when needed. Driving in 4WD at high speeds or on good roads can damage the transmission, steering system, and tires.

A 2WD car can be driven safely through some off-road conditions, if driven properly. Likewise, a 4WD car can become stuck, if not driven properly. Always drive carefully, and slow down if the road conditions are not good.

Avoid Getting Stuck

Each driving situation is unique and your driving experience may determine if you can avoid getting stuck. You must decide when to speed up, when to slow down, when to go, when to stop, when to drive over an obstacle, or when to go around it. Road conditions change quickly and you must react accordingly to avoid an accident.

Ground Clearance

Ground clearance is the distance from the road to the bottom of the car. A car with high ground clearance can be driven over some obstacles, such as a rock or deep snow. Skid plates can be bolted onto the bottom of the car to protect the engine, transmission, and fuel tank from damage.

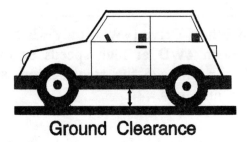

Ground Clearance

High ground clearance can make the car top-heavy and hard to control, especially at high speeds and while turning.

Tire Size & Tread

Large diameter tires increase the ground clearance. Wide tires provide more traction, or gripping ability, and prevent the car from sinking into a soft road surface. Tires with deep tread also increase traction. Tire chains can be used on snow, ice, or mud, for additional traction.

Large tires with deep tread may make humming noises while driving fast. These tires wear rapidly if driven on paved roads at high speeds.

Car Weight

Both the total weight of the car and the location of the weight are important. Normally, the lighter cars are best. A light car will not sink into the soft road surface as quickly and requires less power to move. However, the heavier car usually have larger engine and therefore, more power available.

The weight of the car should be near the drive wheels. A front wheel drive car has most of the weight (engine and transmission) located between the front driving wheels and therefore, usually has very good traction.

Adding weight to the rear of a 2WD truck may increase the traction on the rear wheels.

Driving Off-Road

All roads are bumpy, but some are bumpier than others. Bumps can either be above the road, such as a rock, glass bottle, tree limb; or below the road such as a pothole or gully.

Avoid Hitting The Bump

Either drive around the bump or over the bump. Watch out for other cars and hazards near the road. Try not to look at the bump. Look where you want the tires to go. Staring at the bump can cause you to hit it.

Slow Down

Slow down and drive straight over the bump. Hitting a bump when the car is turning can cause the steering wheel to spin and the car may go out of control. The steering wheel could break your fingers. The faster the car is moving, the less time you have to see the bump and to avoid it.

Wet Roads

Water (rain) will make any road slippery, but some roads can become very slippery. When it first starts to rain, the road may be very slippery because of the oily film on the road surface. Water splashed onto a gasoline engine can cause the engine to sputter or stop. Slow down when driving through water. More stopping distance is needed on a wet road and rain can reduce your visibility.

Hydroplaning

When it rains very hard, the water may not drain off of the road quickly. Cars traveling fast can begin to hydroplane. In other words, the car slides along on a layer of water without actually touching the road surface. When a car hydroplanes, the steering wheel and brakes may not work properly because the tires are not making good contact with the road. Worn or underinflated tires are more likely to cause the car to hydroplane.

Ice

In cold weather, water can freeze and form ice on the road. The tires will have very little traction on ice and the car can slide easily. It is difficult to get the car to move (when it is stopped) or to get the car to stop (if it is moving). Use tire chains or snow tires when driving on ice or snow.

Ice forms first on bridges or shady spots. Use extra caution when driving in cold weather.

Soft Roads

Mud, sand, and snow are common soft road surfaces. The tires will actually sink into the soft road, and therefore the car is not driving on the road, but actually through the road. If the car sinks into the road, the bottom of the car may touch the road and the car can become stuck. High ground clearance will help prevent the bottom of the car from touching the road.

Do not let the tires spin. When the tires spin, they sink into the road deeper and cannot push (or pull) the car very well. When driving on a soft road, move the fuel pedal very slowly. If the tires start to spin, ease back on the fuel pedal (reduce power) until they stop spinning. Spinning tires may get hot and be damaged.

Drive slowly, but keep the car moving. Do not drive too fast, because the car may hit some unseen object. If the car begins to speed up, ease back on the fuel pedal (reduce power). Do not drive too slow, because the car may sink into the soft road. If the car begins to slow down, press the fuel pedal gently to give the engine more power. If the car stops moving, you are stuck. Release the fuel pedal. Do not spin the tires.

Drive in a straight line, if possible. Turning the front wheels may cause the tires to sink down into the soft road faster. Ruts (parallel ditches) are where other cars have driven. If the car has adequate ground clearance, drive with the tires in the ruts because the ruts usually offer better traction. If the car does not have adequate ground clearance, carefully straddle the ruts.

When The Car Is Stuck

Use 4 Wheel Drive. Shift into 4 Wheel Low (4WL). Be sure the hubs are locked. Note: shift into 4WD before the car gets stuck.

Back up. If the car gets stuck going up a hill, back down and try again. Avoid rocking the car back-and-forth, this can damage the transmission.

Stop and inspect the situation. Sometimes just getting the passengers out of the car and having them push will get the car moving again.

Wait for help. If the car is really stuck or damaged, wait for help to arrive or send for help. Use a winch to pull the car out.

4-Wheel Drive & Locking Hubs

Most cars use only two wheels to push (or pull) the car for normal driving conditions. Off-road driving may require extra gripping power or traction to avoid getting stuck. 4 Wheel Drive (4WD) allows all four wheels to push (or pull) the car. A 4WD car will have a second transmission shifting lever (button) needed to shift to/from 4WD.

Know how to use the 4WD correctly and use 4WD only when necessary. Do not wait until the car is stuck before shifting into 4WD.

4WD Shifting Positions

2WH - 2 Wheel High - Normal driving

4WH - 4 Wheel High - Slippery fast driving

4WL - 4 Wheel Low - Maximum Traction

N - Neutral - Operating the PTO or Winch

When driving in 4WD, the steering wheel may be harder to turn because the front wheels are also pulling the car. The car should have a 4WD warning light to indicate when the transmission is in 4WD.

If the 4WD transmission lever is in Neutral (N), the car will not move even if the other shifting lever is moved to (D) Drive or 1st Gear. The Neutral position is used for operating the winch.

Locking Hubs

The hub is the center of the wheel where it connects to the axle. A 4WD car can have front hubs which can be locked when 4WD is needed or released (free) when driving in 2WD. Lock the hubs only when 4WD is needed. The hubs must be in the LOCK position to use 4WD.

Manual Locking Hubs

Manual locking hubs must be adjusted by hand. Driving in 2WD with the hubs locked can waste fuel and damage the transmission. You must stop the car and get out to adjust the hubs.

Automatic Locking Hubs

Automatic locking hubs shift from lock to unlock automatically when the transmission is shifted to/from 4WD. This type of hub offers the most convenience for the driver, while at the same time saving fuel and preventing transmission damage.

When shifting back into 2WD, some cars with automatic locking hubs must move backwards about 10 feet to release the hubs. If this is not done, the hubs can be damaged.

Full Time 4WD

Full time 4WD cars have hubs which are always locked. This is practical only for places where 4WD is used very often. Driving at fast speeds on smooth roads with the hubs locked can waste fuel and damage the transmission or tires.

Additional 4WD Considerations

When compared to a standard 2WD car, the 4WD car will have higher initial cost, operating cost, and maintenance cost. A 4WD car will also not perform as well as a similar 2WD model.

Do not use 4WD on a smooth road at high speeds. This can damage the transmission or tires and waste fuel. Provide proper maintenance to the extra car parts, such as the transfer case, universal joints, and differential. Even if the owners manual says you can shift to/from 4WD while driving, stop or slow down when shifting.

If you seldom drive on rough roads, consider installing a winch on your 2WD car instead of buying a 4WD car.

Most 4WD cars and trucks on the road today are rarely driven on off-road conditions.

Crossing Deep Water

Do not drive through water deeper than the top of the car tires. If the water is moving (river), do not drive through water deeper than 1/2 the height of the tires.

If you are unfamiliar with the water crossing, stop and check for the best route. Have someone walk through the water to look for unseen holes or rocks.

Turn OFF all electric accessories, such as the air conditioner, radio, lights, etc. If water gets inside these items while they are ON, they may be damaged.

Some cars have a removable plug which should be installed in the bottom of the clutch when crossing deep water and removed for normal driving. Check the owners manual.

Be sure the air filter will not get wet. If water gets inside the air filter, serious engine damage will occur.

Use 4 Wheel Low (4WL) to drive slowly through the water while keeping the engine speed around 3000 RPMs. If the engine speed (RPM) is too slow, the engine may stop because the exhaust pipe outlet is under water. If the engine stops, it may not restart.

Test the brakes and check the warning lights and gauges after crossing through the water. Wet brake pads do not work properly. Press the brake pedal lightly while the car is moving to dry the pads.

Crossing A Narrow Bridge

If you are unfamiliar with the bridge crossing, stop the car and check the condition of the bridge. Walk across the bridge to check for unseen holes or broken sections.

Is the bridge strong enough? Make needed repairs to the bridge or unload some of the passengers and cargo to make the car lighter.

Is the bridge wide enough? Measure the distance between the front tires of the car and then check the width of the bridge.

Is the car small enough? Measure the width and height of the car and then check the bridge.

A few minutes needed to inspect the bridge could prevent serious damage to the car or personal injuries.

Using A Winch

A winch is used for pulling. When choosing a winch, consider both the pulling capacity of the winch and the strength of the cable, chain, or rope. The winch must be attached securely to the car and used properly to avoid an accident.

Cables, chains, and ropes are rated according to both the breaking point (ultimate strength) and working strength. The working strength is normally 1/5 of the breaking point. Do not exceed the working strength rating.

Block and Tackle

Block and tackle (pulleys) can multiply the pulling force created by a winch. A small winch with several pulleys and a long cable can exert the same force of a larger winch without the pulleys.

Electric Winch

The electric winch is a small electric motor which uses power from the car battery. The electric winch can be easily installed or removed from the car or can be installed on another car if the electrical system is the same (usually 12 volts). The battery must have adequate power to operate an electric winch.

Engine Powered Winch

The engine powered winch is connected to the transmission of the car with a special drive shaft. This type of winch is sometimes referred to as a PTO (Power Take Off). Power from the engine turns the drive shaft, which turns the winch. The engine must be running to operate this winch.

Hydraulic Winch

A hydraulic winch uses hydraulic pressure, or fluid pressure, to operate the winch. The hydraulic winch is operated by a hydraulic pump (similar to the power steering pump). The engine turns the pump with a belt which forces fluid through small tubes to the winch. This pressurized fluid turns the winch with great force. A car with a hydraulic winch will have an extra belt on the engine and an extra reservoir of hydraulic fluid. The engine must be running to operate the hydraulic winch.

Manual Winch

The manual winch or "come-along" is usually not permanently attached to the car. A handle or lever is moved back-and-forth (or circular motion) to operate the winch. The manual winch is light, portable, and cheap. The engine does not have to be running; however, since it is rather small it may not be able to pull large cars without the use of very long cables and extra pulleys.

Towing A Car

A wire cable is usually used with a winch, but chains and ropes can also be used to pull a car. Keep cables and chains arranged neatly to avoid damage. Extra cables, chains, and ropes should be arranged in 15 to 25 feet lengths with hooks at both ends.

Short pieces of chain (one foot long) should be used to connect the longer pieces of cable, chain, or rope. Any cable, chain, or rope is only a strong as its weakest link. A knot, kink, or worn spot will reduce the working strength and can cause it to break suddenly.

Do not attach two hooks together or tie a cable or chain into a knot, which may damage the hooks, cable, or chain. Always insert a chain into a hook.

Do not use a cable, chain, or rope that is very worn or has knots, kinks, or damaged parts.

These cables, chains, and ropes have about the same working strength (2500 lbs) and breaking point (10,000 lbs).

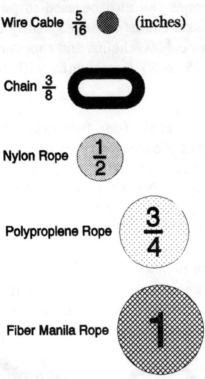

Wire Cable $\frac{5}{16}$ (inches)

Chain $\frac{3}{8}$

Nylon Rope $\frac{1}{2}$

Polyproplene Rope $\frac{3}{4}$

Fiber Manila Rope 1

Check the cable, chain, or rope carefully for cuts, cracks, or other damage. If the rope breaks while you are towing the car, serious damage or personal injuries may result.

Do not exceed the working strength of the rope; it might break suddenly.

Attaching A Tow Rope

Attach the tow rope to either a tow hook or to the frame of the car. Check to be sure the tow rope will not damage any other parts when it is pulled tight. Do not stand near the tow rope when it is towing the car.

> Do not attach the tow rope to the bumpers, axles, steering parts, tie-down hooks, or the suspension system of a car. Make towing hooks from 1/2 steel rods and weld them to the frame of the car, if necessary.

When using a winch attached to the car, attach the end of the cable to an sturdy object such as a large tree, rock, or another car. If no sturdy object is available, attach the cable to a rock (or log) and then put the rock into a deep hole. A boat anchor may be used in some situations. Stay away from the cable while operating the winch.

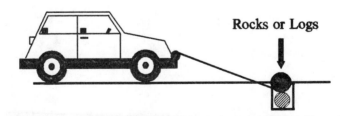

Rocks or Logs

Towing A Car

You should call a tow truck, if possible. It might cost more, but you will avoid damage to the car. You might also push the car out of the way and leave it until you can arrange to have it towed.

If you decide to tow the car with a rope, be sure to attach the tow rope properly. Test the brakes on the car being towed. It must be able to stop without hitting the other car.

Drive slowly, keeping the tow rope tight. Avoid sudden starts, stops and sharp turns. Do not tow a large car behind a small car. This can damage the smaller car.

MAINTENANCE

Maintaining your car in good conditions requires good driving habits and regular maintenance. Both of these are important in reducing the need for major repairs. Regular maintenance ensures that the car is in safe and reliable condition. Newer cars may have fewer maintenance needs than older cars; however, all cars need regular preventive maintenance to avoid major repairs. Learn about the specific maintenance needs for your car and perform frequent visual inspections.

Preventive maintenance and good driving habits are the best ways to keep your car running great for a long time.

General Maintenance Tips

Maintenance depends on the road conditions, your driving habits, and the speed you drive. Check the guidelines in the owners manual. The time limits (ie. week, month, year) are more important and easily remembered than the number of miles driven. Long trips driven at a constant speed are easy on the car compared to the shorter stop-n-go city driving. Refer to Chapter 2 for a list of parts and tools needed for basic maintenance.

> Use the **severe service** maintenance guidelines in the owners manual or divide the standard recommendations by 1/2 (twice as often).

Maintenance

Maintenance is basically replacing certain worn parts before they break. The if-its-not-broken-don't-fix-it attitude can result in a major repair. Replacing a worn out part is usually quicker, easier, and less expensive than replacing the same part that has broken and caused additional damage to other parts.

Whichever maintenance program you use, just do it. Remember to keep a logbook of any maintenance or repairs done to your car.

WEEKLY Maintenance

1. Check Tire Pressure (including Spare)
2. Check Engine Oil level
3. Check Brake Fluid level
4. Check Clutch Fluid level
5. Check Radiator Fluid level
6. Check Automatic Transmission Fluid level
7. Check Power Steering Fluid level
8. Check Windshield Washer Fluid level
9. Check Lights and Turn Signals
10. Check Tool Kit and First Aid Kit
11. Run Air Conditioner (10 minutes)
12. Run Heater (10 minutes)
13. Clean car

Add more clean fluids, as needed. Fill to the FULL mark. Do not overfill. Adjust or repair items, as needed.

Check the owners manual for other items needed for your car. These quick checks will enable you to catch minor problems before car damage results.

Refer to the appropriate sections in this book or the owners manual for the proper way to check, test, or inspect these items.

2-MONTH Maintenance (3000 miles max.)

1. Check Tire Pressure - Spare Tire, too
2. Replace Oil and Oil Filter
3. Lubricate Suspension and Car Body
4. Check Brake Fluid level
5. Check Radiator Fluid level
6. Inspect Engine Belts
7. Inspect Radiator Hoses
8. Inspect Battery
9. Inspect Seat Belts
10. Calculate Fuel Economy or MPG

MPG = (Miles driven) / (Gal. of fuel used).
When the fuel economy drops by more than 10% (about 3 or 5 MPG decrease), the engine may need a tune-up.

If you need to get under the car to inspect or repair any item, use a jackstand to support the weight of the car.

Do not get under a car when it is supported on a jack.

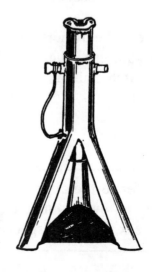

Oil and Filter

Replacing the oil and filter helps prevent engine damage. Use a good quality oil and filter. Recycle the old engine oil.

Lubricate Car Body

Newer cars have fewer grease fittings, however, check the shop manual to be sure. Lubricate the hinges, latches, and linkages.

Engine Belts

If the belt slips, tighten it. Do not over-tighten the belt(s), which will damage the belt or pulleys.

Engine Hoses

Check for cracked or swollen hoses which might break. Look for leaks in the radiator system near the clamps.

Battery

The battery should be secure. The terminal connections should be clean and tight.

Seat belts

Check the belts for damage or wear.

6-MONTH Maintenance (9000 miles max.)

1. Check Tire Pressures - Spare Tire, too
2. Rotate and Balance Tires
3. Inspect Brakes Pads and Brake System
4. Check Wheel Bearings
5. Check Steering System
6. Check Universal Joints or C.V. Joints
7. Test Shock Absorbers and Springs
8. Replace Oil and Oil Filter
9. Lubricate Suspension and Car Body
10. Clean Carburetor and Choke
11. Check Transmission Fluid level
12. Check Transfer Case Oil level (4WD)
13. Check Differential Oil level (RWD)
14. Inspect Rubber Bushings
15. Adjust Clutch (Manual)
16. Adjust Engine Valves (Not Hydraulic)
17. Inspect Engine Belts
18. Inspect Radiator Hoses
19. Check Radiator Fluid Level
20. Inspect Seat Belts
21. Drain Fuel Filter (Diesel)
22. Wash and Polish the Car
23. Calculate Fuel Economy or MPG

If your car has a standard ignition system, do the following two items:

24. Replace Points and Condenser
25. Adjust Timing

Most newer cars have an electronic ignition system and do not have Points or Condenser. Therefore, if your car has electronic ignition, you do not have to replace these items or adjust the timing.

A good time to do this checklist is in the fall. Be sure your car is ready for the cold weather.

Checking Fluids

Use the fill plug to check the level of oil in the manual transmission, differential, and transfer case.

Adjust Engine Valves

Newer cars have hydraulic valves which do not need adjustments. If, however, your car does not have hydraulic engine valves, have them checked and adjusted every 6 months.

Polish The Car

Check the local auto parts store for a good quality car polish. Some compounds contain abrasive material, which may smooth small scratches, but can also scratch some newer car paint finishes.

YEARLY Maintenance (18,000 miles max.)

1. Check Tire Pressures - Spare Tire, too
2. Rotate and Balance Tires
3. Inspect Brakes Pads and Brake System
4. Check Wheel Bearings
5. Check Steering System
6. Check Universal Joints or C.V. Joints
7. Test Shock Absorbers and Springs
8. Replace Oil and Oil Filter
9. Lubricate Suspension and Car Body
10. Clean Carburetor and Choke
11. Replace Air Filter
12. Replace Fuel Filter(s)
13. Replace PCV valve and PCV Filter
14. Replace Sparkplugs
15. Replace Distributor Cap and Rotor
16. Inspect Vacuum Lines
17. Adjust Engine Valves (Not Hydraulic)
18. Inspect Timing Belt / Chain
19. Adjust Engine Idle Speed & Timing
20. Replace Transmission Fluid (Filter)
21. Replace Transfer Case Oil (4WD)
22. Replace Differential Oil (RWD)
23. Adjust Clutch (Manual)
24. Inspect Rubber Bushings
25. Inspect Engine Belts
26. Drain Fuel Filter (Diesel)
27. Wash and Polish the Car
28. Preform State Safety Inspection

29. Inspect Radiator Hoses
30. Check Radiator Fluid Level
31. Add Rust Inhibitor / Water Pump
    Lubricant to Expansion Tank

(Standard Ignition Systems Only)
32. Replace Points and Condenser

Adjust, replace, or repair items according to the shop manual, as needed. Most items a general mechanic can do easily. Several items must be done by a qualified mechanic or technician who has the proper training and tools to avoid serious car damage or injuries.

A good time for this annual checklist is the spring. After a winter of cold weather driving conditions, be sure your car is ready for the summer heat. Divide this list into several smaller list, some items for the tire store, some for the general mechanic, some items you might want to do yourself. Regardless of how you do it, just be sure your car gets complete service and stays in safe operating condition

---

The Annual Checklist should be done on ODD years or when the car is 1 year, 3 years, 5 years, 7 years, 9 years old, etc.

Air Filter

The engine needs 10,000 gallons of air for every gallon of gasoline. Replace the air filter more often in dusty areas. Do not clean or reuse a dirty filter.

Fuel Filter

The fuel filter removes dirt and water which can damage the engine. Some cars have two filters. Fuel injected engines have larger and more expensive fuel filters.

PCV Valve

Positive Crankcase Ventilation valves help remove dangerous vapors from inside the engine to prevent air pollution and increase fuel economy. The PCV valve usually has a filter.

Sparkplugs

Check the owners manual or information under the hood for recommended size and type of sparkplugs. Use a round tool to adjust the gap. Avoid using "hot" plugs which can damage the engine.

Timing Belt

A rubber timing belt is used on many engine to control the engine valves. It is self-adjusting, but should be checked every year and replaced about every 4 years. Some engines have a metal timing chain.

Transmission Fluid

Replace the manual transmission oil or automatic transmission fluid and filter. Some automatic transmissions are equipped with a reusable permanent filter.

Rubber Bushings

Check for damage to the rubber bushings. Look for cracks or broken bushings on the suspension system or engine.

Rust Inhibitor / Water Pump Lubricant

Add a can of rust inhibitor and water pump lubricant to the expansion tank. This will keep the radiator system clean and operating properly. If the radiator fluid is over 2 years old or dirty, change it.

2-YEAR Maintenance (36,000 miles max.)

1. Check Tire Pressures - Spare Tire, too
2. Rotate and Balance Tires
3. Inspect Brakes Pads and Brake System
4. Replace Brake Fluid
5. Check Wheel Bearings
6. Check Steering System
7. Check Universal Joints or C.V. Joints
8. Test Shock Absorbers and Springs
9. Adjust Wheel Alignment
10. Replace Oil and Oil Filter
11. Lubricate Suspension and Car Body
12. Clean Carburetor and Choke
13. Replace Air Filter
14. Replace Fuel Filter(s)
15. Replace PCV valve and PCV Filter
16. Replace Sparkplugs
17. Replace Distributor Cap and Rotor
18. Inspect Vacuum Lines
19. Adjust Engine Valves (Not Hydraulic)
20. Inspect Timing Belt / Chain
21. Adjust Engine Idle Speed and Timing
22. Replace Transmission Fluid (Filter)
23. Replace Transfer Case Oil (4WD)
24. Replace Differential Oil (RWD)
25. Replace Clutch Fluid (Manual)
26. Adjust Clutch (Manual)
27. Inspect Rubber Bushings
28. Inspect Engine Belts
29. Inspect Radiator Hoses

30. Replace Radiator Fluid
31. Replace Power Steering Fluid
32. Drain Fuel Filter (Diesel)
33. Wash and Polish the Car
34. Preform State Safety Inspection
35. Service Air Conditioner System
36. Replace Windshield Wipers or Inserts

(Standard Ignition Systems Only)
37. Replace Points and Condenser

Make Several Shorter Lists

 The 2 Year Checklist may seem rather long, but remember that everything does not need to be done at one time. Many of these items might not apply to your car, or your car might have other items not listed here. Make several shorter lists, but be sure to do all the necessary items.

 If you want your car to last a long time and stay in safe operating condition, preventive maintenance will help avoid a major costly repair.

The 2 Year Checklist should be done when the car is 2 Years, 6 Years, 10 Years old, etc.

4-YEAR Maintenance (72,000 miles max.)

1. Check Tire Pressures - Spare Tire, too
2. Rotate and Balance Tires
3. Inspect Brakes Pads and Brake System
4. Replace Brake Fluid
5. Check Wheel Bearings
6. Check Steering System
7. Check Universal Joints or C.V. Joints
8. Test Shock Absorbers and Springs
9. Adjust Wheel Alignment
10. Replace Oil and Oil Filter
11. Lubricate Suspension and Car Body
12. Clean Carburetor and Choke
13. Replace Air Filter
14. Replace Fuel Filter(s)
15. Replace PCV valve and PCV Filter
16. Replace Sparkplugs
17. Replace Sparkplug Wires
18. Replace Distributor Cap and Rotor
19. Inspect Vacuum Lines
20. Check Pollution Control Systems
21. Replace Timing Belt
22. Adjust Engine Valves (Not Hydraulic)
23. Adjust Engine Idle Speed and Timing
24. Replace Transmission Fluid (Filter)
25. Replace Transfer Case Oil (4WD)
26. Replace Differential Oil (RWD)
27. Replace Clutch Fluid (Manual)
28. Adjust Clutch (Manual)
29. Inspect Rubber Bushings

30. Replace Engine Belts
31. Replace Radiator Hoses and Clamps
32. Replace Radiator Fluid
33. Replace Radiator Cap
34. Replace Thermostat
35. Replace Water Pump
36. Replace Fuel Cap
37. Test Fuel Pump
38. Replace Power Steering Fluid
39. Drain Fuel Filter (Diesel)
40. Wash and Polish the Car
41. Preform State Safety Inspection
42. Service A/C system
43. Replace Windshield Wipers or Inserts
44. Replace Battery
45. Inspect Battery Cables

(Standard Ignition Systems Only)
46. Replace Points and Condenser

Special Notes On The 4 Year Checklist

Four years is a critical time in the life of your automobile. After four years of driving, the car needs special attention in order to continue operating properly.

Check the owners manual and shop manual for any special maintenance needed for your car. Refer to the shop manual for specific test or repair instructions.

Although this checklist is the longest and most expensive, it will keep your car running great for many more miles and greatly reduce the cost-per-mile of owning the car. You do not have to do all items at one time, however, some items should be grouped together to save time and money.

Warning: If you neglect or postpone the maintenance, your car can develop serious problems which will require more expensive repairs.

Preventive maintenance reduces the overall cost-per-mile of owning a car.

Pollution Control Systems

The car may be equipped with pollution control systems that need to be repaired or replaced about every 50,000 miles.

Water Pump

The water pump must be removed to replace the rubber timing belt. Therefore, have the water pump and timing belt replaced at the same time.

Wheel Alignment

The wheels must be in the correct position to provide the longest tire life and good fuel economy. All cars need a front wheel alignment, however, some cars need the rear wheels aligned, too. Check the alignment when buying new tires, having the struts replaced, after any accident, or when the tires do not wear evenly.

Battery

Replace the battery every 4 years, before it dies and cannot start the engine. Be sure the battery is installed correctly. Do not over tighten the battery which can damage the metal plates inside. Install anti-corrosion washers to prevent corrosion.

Brake Hoses

Carefully inspect the flexible brake hoses located near each wheel. These hoses need to be replaced, if they are damaged.

Thermostat

The thermostat has a temperature stamped on it. This is the temperature it will start to open, not the engine operating temperature. Be sure you purchase the right thermostat for your car.

Radiator Cap

The radiator cap spring may weaken after several years and not hold the proper pressure inside the cooling system. This can cause the engine to overheat. Replace the cap.

Fuel Cap

The fuel cap vent can get clogged. This can cause the engine to run rough or pollute the atmosphere. Replace the cap.

The 4 Year Checklist is long, but it is needed only twice for most cars (at 4 and 8 years) and is much less expensive than buying a new car.

TROUBLE SHOOTING

Newer cars are much more complex, yet in some ways they are easier to maintain and repair. If you plan to do any maintenance or repairs yourself, invest in a shop manual for your car. These manuals are available at local libraries or bookstores. If you cannot find one, ask the dealership to order one for you. They cover every part and procedure for your car. Always read the directions carefully and take your time when repairing the car. Using cheap tools, getting in a hurry, or skipping important steps can cause injuries or car damage.

Repairing a car properly requires tools, parts, and information. Regular maintenance can prevent most common car problems.

Changing A Flat Tire

1. Park the car in a safe level spot. Apply the parking brake and turn the key switch to OFF. Put blocks both in front and behind two tires (not the flat tire). Passengers should get out.

2. Put the spare tire, jack, and tool kit near the flat tire.

3. Remove the wheel cover (hubcap), if necessary.

4. Using the lug wrench or tire tool, loosen each lugnut about one turn. Do not remove them. Turn most lugnuts Counter Clock Wise (left) to remove them.

5. Place the jack securely on solid ground under the frame of the car and raise the car until the flat tire is about three inches off the ground.

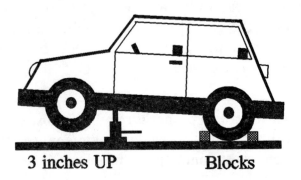

3 inches UP   Blocks

6. Remove the lugnuts from the flat tire. Then remove the flat tire.

7. Put the spare tire onto the wheel and install the lugnuts. Tighten the lugnuts snugly, using a criss-cross pattern. Do not over-tighten the lugnuts until the car is lowered and the wheel is touching the ground. Over-tightening could cause the car to roll off the jack.

8. Lower the car until the spare tire touches the ground. Do not remove the jack.

9. Use a criss-cross pattern to tighten the lugnuts. The criss-cross pattern tightens the tire evenly and prevents it from coming loose.

10. Remove the jack.

11. Place the flat tire, jack, and all the tools in the car and drive to the nearest repair shop to get the flat tire repaired. Do not drive faster than 45 MPH or more than 45 miles while using a compact spare tire.

90% of tire problems occur during the final 10% of the tire life, or after the wear-bars show. Don't drive on worn tires.

The Engine Does Not Start

If the key switch does not move, turn the steering wheel slightly while turning the key into position. If the engine does not make any noise, check the safety starting switches.

When the key switch is turned to START, the engine may not turn and you will hear clicking sounds. The battery may be very weak or the battery cable connections are corroded or loose.

Turn the headlights and A/C OFF. Try starting the engine. Check the battery cable connections. Clean and tighten the cable connections. Check the cable connections at the starter and car frame, too.

If the battery is dead or the starter is damaged, the engine may start with a jumpstart.

Jumpstart

When the battery is "dead" or has very little power, the engine may not start. A jumpstart is when booster cables are connected to a charged battery to provide more power to the dead battery.

Improper jumper-cable connections can cause serious injuries and car damage. Use caution and wear eye protection.

Turn the headlights OFF when the engine is not running to avoid a dead battery.

Before attempting to jumpstart, check the automatic transmission shifting lever and safety starting switches. The lever must be in (P) Park or (N) Neutral.

Both batteries must be about the same size and have the same voltage. Do not jumpstart a very cold battery.

1. Check the level of battery fluid in both batteries. Add distilled water, if necessary.

2. Position the cars so that the jumper-cables can reach both batteries eas_ly. Do not allow the cars to touch each other. Apply the parking brakes firmly in both cars. Turn both engines OFF.

3. Disconnect both battery terminal cables (NEGative first) from the good battery. This will protect the ignition systems in both cars.

225

4. Turn the A/C and headlights OFF in the car with the dead battery.

There are 4 jumper-cable connections. When installing the cables, make the last connection on the metal frame or engine of the car with the "dead battery". When removing the cables, disconnect the metal frame or engine first. This helps keep any sparks away from the battery.

Jump - Start Connections

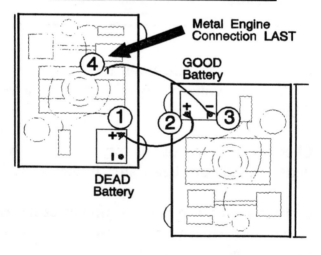

 Do not allow the ends of the jumper-cables to touch each other. This will cause sparks and damage the battery. Never test the battery this way.

5. Connect the positive terminal of the good battery to the positive terminal of the dead battery using the RED jumper-cable.

6. Connect the negative terminal of the good battery to the engine of the car with dead battery using the BLACK jumper-cable.

7. Check the jumper-cables to be sure they are fastened properly and will not touch any moving parts when the engine starts.

8. Try starting the car with the dead battery. Do not operate the starter for more than 10 seconds. If the car does not start after three tries, there may be another problem with the car (besides the dead battery).

9. When the car with the dead battery starts, remove the jumper-cables carefully, starting with the engine connection.

Disconnect

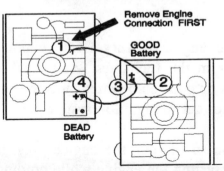

227

10. Allow the engine to run at least 30 minutes to recharge the dead battery.

11. Check the electrical system indicators for indications of electrical system problems.

12. Reconnect the battery cables on the good battery (POSitive cable first).

The Engine Turns Quickly

When the key switch is turned to START, the engine may turn very quickly, but not start. This usually indicates that there is a problem with the ignition system or the fuel system.

1. Check the fuel gauge. If the fuel supply is low, add several gallons of fuel.

2. Loosen the fuel cap. If the cap vent becomes clogged, the fuel pump cannot remove the fuel from the tank because air cannot get into the tank.

3. If the engine is very HOT, vapor lock may occur in the fuel lines. Wait until the engine cools or pour cold water onto the fuel lines. Do not get the ignition system wet.

4. If you smell fuel, the engine may be flooded. Try starting the engine while holding the fuel

pedal all the way down. Do not pump the pedal. If the engine does not start, wait one hour for the excess fuel to evaporate.

5. If the ignition system is wet, dry it off. Check the distributor cap (inside and outside) and the sparkplug wires or wait for the engine to dry.

6. Check the sparkplugs. Clean or replace them, if necessary.

7. Check the fuel pump. Some electric fuel pumps have an circuit breaker switch, which can be reset. Check the fuel lines for damage.

8. Check the air filter and choke. Replace a dirty filter or clean the choke.

The Engine Does Not Run Good

The engine might start, but not run very good. This usually indicates that there is a problem with the ignition system or fuel system. Dirt or water in the fuel can cause temporary engine problems. Always use clean fuel. Change the filter(s) each year.

1. Check the vacuum hoses near the engine. A loose or damaged hose can cause the engine to sputter.

2. If the ignition system is wet, dry it off. Check the distributor cap (inside and outside) and each sparkplug wire, or wait for the engine to dry.

3. Check the sparkplugs.

4. Check the air filter and choke. Replace a dirty filter or clean the choke.

5. Check the exhaust pipes. If they are damaged or clogged, the engine may not run very good.

If the engine runs after the key switch is OFF (dieseling), or if it backfires while driving, adjust the timing on the engine or do a complete tune-up.

The Car Does Not Move

The engine may start and run fine, but the car might not move. This usually indicates that there is a problem with the transmission.

1. Check for objects under the car or near the wheels. Release the parking brake. Note: If the parking brake is applied when the wheels are wet, the brake pads can become stuck. Release the parking brake lever and gently rock the car back and forth to loosen the pads.

2. When the transmission shifting lever will not move, gently push the car back and forth while shifting the lever into position.

3. Check the automatic transmission fluid level. Add more fluid, if necessary, and check for a leak in the transmission.

4. Check the manual clutch fluid level. Add more brake fluid, if necessary, and check for leaks. If the clutch pedal is spongy, bleed the system. Check the clutch adjustment.

5. In a 4 Wheel Drive car, check the 4WD selector. If the 4WD selector is in (N) Neutral, the car will not move. Select (2WH) for normal driving conditions or (4WL) for off-road conditions.

The Car Does Not Stop

When the car moves but does not stop, this indicates a problem with the brakes.

1. Pump the brake pedal and apply the parking brake gently to stop the car. Do not allow the wheels to lock-up.

2. After driving through deep water, the brake pads get wet and may not work properly. Press the brake pedal lightly for several seconds

while the car is moving to dry the pads. Test the brakes after driving in water.

3. Release the brakes. Driving with the parking brake engaged or with your foot on the brake pedal may cause the car to pull to one side and seem to lack power.

4. Check the brake fluid level. Add more clean brake fluid when necessary. If the brake pedal feels spongy, bleed the brake system to remove air. Check for leaks in the brake system.

Have the brakes checked every 6 MONTHS and repaired as needed. Do not drive a car when the brakes do not operate properly.

Smoke & Odors

Both the color and the location of the smoke can indicate the problem.

Engine Smoke

1. Check for oil leaking onto hot engine parts. Tighten the valve cover on top of the engine or replace the valve cover gasket. Replace the PCV valve.

2. If the engine is very HOT, stop the car and turn the engine OFF. Do not open the hood or remove the radiator cap when the engine is HOT.

> When adding oil to the engine, avoid spilling it onto the exhaust pipes.

3. Check the level of coolant in the expansion tank and add water to achieve a FULL level. Check for a broken hose, thermostat, or belt.

> Radiator fluid leaking onto hot car parts can cause a pungent odor.

Gray Exhaust Gas

Some smoke is normal from the exhaust pipe when the engine starts, especially in a diesel engine. Excessive or continuous smoke can indicate a more serious engine problem.

1. Check the level of the engine oil and add more oil to achieve a FULL level. Check the type (viscosity or thickness) of the engine oil.

2. Replace the PCV valve.

Black Exhaust Gas

A rich mixture (too much fuel or too little air) can cause black exhaust gas.

1. Check the air filter. Replace it, if necessary.
2. Clean the choke, carburetor, or fuel injectors.
3. Check the fuel filter(s). Replace it, if necessary.

White Smoke From The Exhaust Pipes

White smoke is steam (water) in the exhaust gases. This can indicate a leak in the cooling system inside the engine. Some steam is a normal part of the exhaust gases and should not cause concern, if the radiator fluid level is normal and the engine does not overheat.

1. Check the level of the radiator fluid in the expansion tank. Add water, if necessary, to maintain a FULL level.

2. Tighten the bolts on the cylinder head with a torque wrench according to the shop manual.

Exhaust Gas Inside The Car

Exhaust gas inside the car can be caused by a leak in the exhaust pipe or a clogged exhaust pipe. Do not breath the exhaust gases, it is poisonous and can cause headache, nausea, and even death.

1. Roll down the windows and get some fresh air.
2. Check the exhaust pipe outlet.
3. Cover the hole which allows the exhaust gas to enter the car.

Burning Plastic Odors

A short circuit can cause the electrical wires to get very hot and melt.

1. Stop the car and turn the key switch to OFF.
2. Disconnect the battery cables (NEGative first).
3. Check the fuse box for a broken fuse.
4. Locate broken or damaged wires.

Burning Rubber Odor

A slipping belt can cause a burning rubber odor.

1. Check the tension of the belts.
2. Inspect the belts for damage.
3. Tighten or replace the belts, if necessary.

Smoke From The Wheels

If the brake pads do not release properly, or if the car is driven with the parking brakes engaged, the brake pads can get very hot and cause smoke.

1. Stop the car.

2. Wait until the wheels cool down before attempting any repairs. Do not drive when the brakes are damaged.

Smoke From Vents Inside The Car

The heater or A/C can produce smoke from the vents inside the car. This can cause the windshield to fog and is normally due to certain temperature or humidity conditions inside the car. Smoke from the vents can sometimes indicate a problem with the heating or A/C system.

1. Check the engine temperature indicator. If the engine temperature is very HOT, then stop the car and turn the key switch to OFF.

2. Check the radiator fluid level in the expansion tank. Add more water, if necessary, to maintain a FULL level.

3. If the A/C does not cool properly, turn it OFF and have it serviced.

Leaking Fluids

Both the color and the location of the leak can determine which fluid is leaking. Most leaks can be stopped by tightening a connection or replacing a gasket.

Black Fluid - Engine Oil

1. Check the engine oil level.
2. Check the oil filter, oil drain plug, oil pan gasket. Replace the PCV valve.

Brown Fluid - Transmission or Differential Oil

1. Look for leaks at the gaskets.
2. Check the transmission and differential oil levels.

Red Fluid - Automatic Transmission Fluid

1. Check the automatic transmission fluid level.
2. Check the power steering fluid level.

Green or Blue Fluid - Radiator Fluid

1. Check the fluid level in the expansion tank.
2. Check the radiator and radiator hoses for leaks.

Clear Fluid

1. Brake fluid can leak from near the wheels or under the hood. Check the fluid level in the brake fluid reservoir and clutch fluid reservoir.

2. Fuel has a very unique odor. Look for leaks near the fuel tank, filter(s), or engine.

3. Battery acid can leak from the battery. Inspect the battery for cracks or damage.

4. Water may drain from under the car when the A/C is operating. This is normal and does not need to be repaired. If water is dripping from under the dashboard inside the car, then check the A/C drain tube connections.

Stopping Leaks

1. Locate the leak.
2. Tighten the connection(s) or repair the hose.
3. Add the proper fluid to the FULL level.

Do not over-tighten the connection(s). Do not overfill the fluid levels.

> Operating the car when any fluid is below the **MINimum** level can cause damage or accidents.

Strange Noises

Both the type of noise and the location of the noise can indicate the type of problem.

Hissing Sounds

1. Check the vacuum hoses near the engine.

2. Check for small leaks (white spots) from the radiator or radiator hoses. Do not touch any hot any engine parts.

Whirling Noises

1. Check the power steering fluid level.
2. Check the transmission and differential oil.
3. Check the universal joints (C.V. Joints)

Dragging Noises

1. Stop the car in a safe place. Apply the parking brakes. Turn the key switch to OFF.

2. Check for objects under the car. Secure or remove any object dragging the ground. Do not touch any hot parts.

3. Check the brake pads. A dragging noise from the wheel can indicate a brake problems.

Clicking Noises

1. Check the engine oil level. Change the engine oil and filter, if necessary. Use the proper viscosity/thickness of oil.

2. Check for a rock in the tire tread or hubcap.

3. Check the hubcaps and lugnuts. Tighten them, as needed.

Squealing Noises

1. Check the belts. Adjust the tension or replace the belt. Do not over-tighten the belt. This can damage the belt and pulleys.

Humming Noises

1. Check the tire pressure with an accurate gauge. Inflate the tire(s) to the proper pressure.

The tire pressure should be measured when the tires are **cold** (before driving). The pressure may increase after driving the car. Do not overinflate.

---

2. Check the tire tread for even wear.

Steering Problems

The steering wheel can shake, or vibrate, if one of the tires is out-of-balance. This may happen at only certain speeds. Properly balanced tires will last much longer.

1. Check the tire tread wear.
2. Have the tires balanced and rotated.
3. Check the steering system.
4. Check the brake drums/rotors.

Steering Wheel Pulls To One Side

1. Release the parking brake.
2. Check the air pressure in all four tires.
3. Have the tire alignment checked.

Steering Wheel Is Loose

1. Check the ball joints and the steering system. Do not drive a car when the steering wheel play is more than 2 inches.

Steering Wheel Is Tight

1. Check the power steering fluid level.
2. Check the belt on the power steering pump.

Warning Lights

Oil Pressure Light

The oil pressure light indicates that there is not adequate oil pressure needed to lubricate the engine. This can be caused by a low engine oil level or the wrong type of oil. Low engine oil pressure can cause serious engine damage. Stop the car and turn the engine OFF.

Engine Temperature Light

The engine temperature light
indicates that the engine is

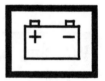

very HOT. This can be caused by
a problem with the engine cooling system
(broken hose, belt, thermostat), or by using the
A/C, driving too fast, poor ignition timing, or low
oil level. High engine temperatures can cause
serious engine damage.

1. Turn the A/C OFF.
2. Turn the heater ON (Heat=HOT, Fan=HIGH).
3. Stop the car and turn the engine OFF.

Battery Light

The battery light indicates that
the battery is not being charged by
the alternator. The car may
continue to run as long as there is
power available in the battery.

1. Turn OFF all unnecessary electrical accessories
   (air conditioner, lights, fans, radio, wipers).

2. Clean and tighten the battery cable
   connections. Check the battery fluid level.

If a burning odor, smoke, or strange noise is
noticed, stop the car and turn the engine OFF.

3. Check the alternator belt and the alternator electrical connections.

4. Check the fuse box and voltage regulator.

Brake Light

1. Release the parking brakes.

2. Check the brake fluid level.

3. Check for a broken brake light bulb.

4. Check the switch adjustment near the brake pedal or the parking brake lever.

If your car has Anti-Lock Brakes, the warning light may indicate some problem with this system. Have the brakes inspected by a qualified technician as soon as possible. If there is any problem with the anti-lock brake system, the brakes should operate in the regular mode, however, the tires may skid if you apply the brakes very hard.

Check Engine Light

This light normally refers to some part of the emission control system. Refer to the owners manual or shop manual for specific information.

Check Filter Light

This light normally refers to the fuel filter or water separator on a diesel engine. Drain about one cup of fuel or/dirt/water from the filter.

CAR ACCIDENTS

If you are involved in an accident, even if you are not injured or your car damaged, you should:

1. Stop and remain at the scene of the accident. If you must leave to seek medical attention or notify the police, return as soon as possible. Do not move the cars, unless this unnecessarily obstructs traffic. Use warning devices to alert other drivers that an accident has occurred.

Do not have heat or sparks near the accident scene. Place "flares" away from the damaged cars, which may leak fuel and cause a fire.

2. Assist the injured. If the person cannot breathe or is bleeding, immediate action is needed in order to save her/his life. Do not move the injured person unless she/he is in immediate danger.

3. Send for help. Call 911 and request an ambulance. The police will make a report describing the accident. Other drivers or witnesses should provide their names, addresses, and phone numbers. Drivers involved in the accident are required to show their drivers license and vehicle registration. The police may request information about your car insurance.

> If you make any statements about the accident, they may be used against you in court. Do not sign anything or make/accept any payment until you understand the consequences and talk to your attorney.

4. See a doctor. Serious injuries are not always obvious at the time of an accident. Describe the accident to a doctor and have a complete examination.

5. Report the accident. Your insurance agent can help you with an accident report. If you need legal assistance, seek the advice of an attorney.

Basic First Aid

Keep a First Aid Kit, including a First Aid Manual, in the car.

If the injured person has head or neck injuries, do not move them unless absolutely necessary.

---

1. Be sure the injured person can breathe. Preform CPR, mouth-to-mouth resuscitation, or the Heimlich Maneuver. If you do not know these important lifesaving techniques, take a course to learn how to do them properly and safely.

2. Be sure the injured person is not bleeding. Apply direct pressure to the wound and elevate the wound slightly to slow the blood flow.

3. Have the injured person lie down in a safe place. Keep her/him warm.

4. Send for help or take the injured person to a doctor. Call 911 or the police and request an ambulance.

Choking

Do not hit the person on the back. Preform the Heimlich Maneuver. For children use less pressure.

Burns

1. For minor burns, use cool water to ease the pain. Then clean the area carefully, but do not break the blisters.

2. Third degree or serious burns require special attention. Take the person to a doctor or hospital.

Broken Bones

1. Immobilize the broken bone with a splint. Do not attempt to set a broken bone.
2. Stop the bleeding.
3. Have the person lie down.
4. Take them to a doctor.

Survival Tips

Survival means staying alive. Regardless of the unfortunate circumstances that cause you to be in a survival situation, you must decide to do what is necessary in order to stay alive. You can be sure that other people with less training than you have been in worse situations and survived. Although no one plans to become stranded, being prepared for a survival situation can mean an earlier rescue and better conditions until help arrives.

When you plan a trip into a very cold, very hot, or very remote area, inform someone of your travel plans and carry an adequate supply of food and water.

Survival Action

1. Provide first aid to the injured.
2. Take time to relax.
3. Develop a survival plan.

A group will have a better chance of surviving if everyone stays together and cooperates.

Signal For Help

Getting help as soon as possible is a primary goal in any survival situation. Send an S-O-S .

```
S-O-S--dot-dot-dot--dash-dash-dash--
dot-dot-dot-dash-dash-dash--. . . .
```

1. The universal distress signal is S-O-S or any signal in sets of **three**. An S-O-S with morse code is made up of three dots followed by three dashes repeated continuously. A dot is any short signal of sound or light. A dash is a longer signal.

2. If there is any chance that someone is within hearing distance of the car, try using the car horn. Sound three short beeps followed by three longer beeps followed by three short beeps. Repeat signal.

3. If there is any chance that someone can see the car, use the headlights to flash a signal.

4. Use a fire at night or smoke during the day to signal for help. Produce dark smoke by burning rubber parts of the car or by adding engine oil to the fire. Three separate fires may attract more attention.

5. If there is a chance that someone may be searching for you from the air, disturb the natural look of the area. Cut down trees, pull up grass or shrubs, fly a colored flag in a tall tree, place bright parts of the car in a clearing.

6. Mirrors, or any shinny object, can also be used to send a signal. Aim the reflection at aircraft or near the horizon. Keep the mirror moving.

Find Shelter

If bad weather is approaching, look for better shelter such as a house, barn, or service station, **before** you become stranded. If you cannot see better shelter, stay in the car. Having protection from the sun, wind, rain, and snow will help you survive until help arrives. Avoid extremes in temperature by controlling your environment as much as possible.

1. Stay in the car. If you cannot stay inside the car, try to stay near the car. Your rescuers will be looking for the car. If you abandon the car, leave a message near the car.

2. Look for natural shelters such as a cave, rocky overhangs, large log. Use parts of the car, such as the hood, trunk, seats, floor mats, to build a small lean-to for shelter. Conserve your energy.

Stay Warm In The Car

If the car becomes stuck in very cold weather, you must take proper precautions to avoid suffocating on the exhaust gases.

1. Make sure the exhaust pipe is clear before starting the engine.

2. Run the engine for 15 minutes with the heater on **HOT** and the fan on **HIGH**. Open one of the windows slightly for some fresh air. Then turn the engine **OFF** for 30 minutes and close the window. If you become sleepy or develop a headache, open the windows for fresh air. Watch the fuel supply.

3. Blow the horn and flash the lights while the engine is running. Watch for rescuers.

4. Use any available material, such as floor mats, seat covers, or roof material, to stay warm. Keep your head covered. Hug another person.

5. Eat food and candy to help your body produce heat. Do not eat snow or ice which may lower your body temperature.

Water

You can survive for weeks without much food, but only days without water. Each person will need about one quart of water every day. During very hot dry weather, each person may need more than four quarts (one gallon) of water every day.

1. Drinking water can be found in the ground, rain, snow, dew, ice, plants, vines, or fruits.

2. Sterilize all water, either by boiling it for 15 minutes or by using iodine or chlorine tablets. Do not conserve drinking water. You will need to drink it sooner or later.

3. In hot weather, reduce water loss from sweating and wind evaporation. Wear light clothing and stay in the shade whenever possible.

Do not drink saltwater, brackish water, radiator fluid, or windshield washer fluid. Special care should be used with radiator fluid which has a sweet taste, but is extremely poisonous.

Fire

Do not have the fire near the car. Gasoline is extremely flammable. Use matches or the cigarette lighter to start a fire. The fire can be used to signal for help, cook food, keep warm, and scare away bugs and wild animals.

1. Keep waterproof matches in the first aid kit. Waterproof some matches by dipping the ends in wax or fingernail polish.

2. Once the fire is burning, keep it going, unless the supply of wood or fuel is very small.

Food

There are two basic types of food: **animal** and **plant**. With very few exceptions, all animals are edible if cooked properly. Smaller animals are usually more plentiful and easier to catch. Many plants, including the leaves, roots, fruits, and nuts, are edible and some are rather tasty; however, some will make you very sick. Do not eat anything with a bitter taste or milky sap.

Items For Remote Areas

1. Food
2. Water
3. Blankets
4. Change of Clothes
5. Waterproof Matches (Lighter)
6. First Aid Kit
7. String
8. Knife
9. Plastic Bags

The most basic items can mean the difference between a difficult situation and a disaster. Hope for the best, but be prepared for the worst.

Enjoy your trip!

GLOSSARY

A

ABS - Antilock Brake System prevents the wheels from locking during sudden stops.

A/C - air conditioning.

Air Cleaner - the metal container which holds the air filter.

Air Filter - the replaceable part inside the air cleaner which removes dirt and dust from the air entering the engine.

Air Pressure Gauge - measures the amount of air inside the tires. PSI = Pounds per Square Inch.

Alternating Current or **AC** - electricity reversing directions (as opposed to flowing in one direction). See direct current.

Alternator - produces electricity needed to charge the battery and operate the accessories in the car.

Ampere or **AMP** - amount of electric current or power.

Antifreeze - see coolant.

Automatic Transmission Fluid or **ATF** - hydraulic fluid in the automatic transmission and power steering system.

B

Ball Joint - flexible connection on the steering or suspension system. See tie rod.

Battery - a plastic box containing metal plates in acid and water. The battery stores electrical power (12 Volts).

Belt - a flexible rubber belt on the engine. See timing belt.

Bearing - the part used to reduce friction between two moving parts. Bearings are found inside the engine, transmission, or near each wheel.

Black Box - any electronic device which cannot be adjusted or repaired.

Bleeding - removing air bubbles from the hydraulic system.

Blue Book Value - Calculating the standard cost of a used car, based on the age, mileage, and condition of the car.

Boot - a rubber cover used to keep out dirt and water.

Brake Fluid - a special fluid used in the brake or clutch system.

Brake Pads - the replaceable part of the brake which is pressed against a rotating metal surface to slow or stop the car. Also called brake shoes. See disc and drum brakes.

Bushing - a rubber part which absorbs vibrations and reduces rattles.

C

Caliper - the part of the disc brake which pushes the brake pads against the rotating disc.

Camber - a measurement of the wheel alignment.

Carburetor - a method of mixing the gasoline with air so it can be burned inside the engine. See also fuel injection.

Caster - a measurement of the wheel alignment.

Catalytic Converter - a part of the exhaust system used reduce harmful pollution.

CCA or Cold Cranking Amps - an estimate of the power in a battery when it is cold.

Centrifugal Advance - adjusting the timing of the engine with small rotating weights. See also vacuum advance.

Choke - used to start a cold engine. The choke limits the air entering the engine and produces a richer (more fuel) mixture.

Clutch - the connection between the engine and transmission.

Coil - boost the low battery voltage (12 volts) to a high voltage (20,000 volts) needed for the sparkplugs.

Compression Test - an easy way to check the internal condition of an engine. If the compression is low, major repairs may be needed.

Coolant - chemical mixed with water to make radiator fluid. The coolant, or anti-freeze, lubricates the cooling system, prevents rust, and helps prevent overheating and freezing.

Criss-Cross - a method of tightening opposite lug nuts to insure that the wheel is tight.

C.V. Joint - Constant Velocity Joint is the flexible connection on the ends of a drive shaft. See universal joint.

CW - **Clock Wise** - turning to the RIGHT or the direction a clock hand moves in order to tighten parts.

CCW - **Counter Clock Wise** turning to the LEFT or the opposite direction a clock hand moves to loosen parts.

D

Dead Battery - a battery without power to start the engine.

Dieseling - an engine which continues to run after the key switch is turned to OFF.

Differential - part of the transmission which allows the wheels to turn smoothly in a curve.

Dipstick - used to measure a fluid level.

Direct Current or **DC** - electrical power flowing in only one direction, such as a battery. See alternating current.

Disc Brake - a flat rotating disc (rotor) with a stationary caliper and flat brake pads. Normally used on the front wheels.

Distributor Cap - the removable top part of the distributor where the spark plugs wires are attached.

Down Shifting - slowing the car or increasing the engine speed by shifting into a lower gear.

Drive Train - parts of the car located between the engine and the drive wheels: clutch, transmission, differential, drive shafts, and universal (or CV) joints.

Drum Brake - a curved rotating drum with a stationary wheel cylinder and curved brake pads. Normally used on the rear wheels where the parking brake is attached.

E

EGR or **Exhaust Gas Recirculating Valve** - part of the emission controls needed to reduce air pollution.

Electrical System Indicators - warning light, ammeter, or voltmeter.

Electronic Ignition System - an expensive, but reliable, type of ignition system that does not use points or condensers. See also black boxes.

Engine Temperature Indicators - the temperature gauge or warning light used to indicate the engine temperature.

Expansion Tank - the reservoir for excess radiator fluid.

Evaporator - a small radiator under the dashboard needed for the A/C system.

F

Fading - when the brakes (drum) get very hot and cannot stop the car after heavy use.

Fan - forces air through the radiator to cool the radiator fluid and keep the engine from overheating.

Float or **Float Valve** - parts inside the carburetor used to regulate the flow of gasoline to the engine.

Flooding - too much fuel (or not enough air) at the engine, which will cause it not to start.

Four Wheel Drive or **4WD** - using all four wheels for extra traction to pull or push the car.

Free Play - see play.

Friction - resistance to motion between two surfaces. Oil is used inside the engine to reduce friction and heat.

Front Wheel Drive or **FWD** - using the front wheels to the pull the car.

Fuel-Air Mixture - the mixture burned inside the engine to produce the power needed to turn the engine and move the car.

Fuel Filter - removes dirt and water from the fuel before it enters the engine.

Fuel Injection - mixing the fuel and air by squirting fuel directly into the engine. Used on both gasoline and diesel engines. See also carburetor.

Fuel Pedal - controls the power and speed of the engine.

Fuel Pump - a small pump needed to move the fuel from the tank to the engine. May be electric (in the tank) or mechanical (on the engine).

Fuse - the "weak-link" to protect the electrical system from excessive power.

Fuse Box - a central location for the fuses.

Fusible Link - a small piece of wire or metal placed in a main circuit which melts and acts like a fuse.

G

Gap - the distance between the electrodes on a sparkplug as measured with a round gauge.

Gasket - a soft material used to form an airtight seal between two surfaces.

Gears - part of the transmission needed for increasing the speed of the car.

Glow Plugs - needed to start a cold diesel engine.

Grease - a very thick lubricant used on some bearings and the suspension.

Grease Fitting - is where a grease gun can be attached to add grease. See ball joint.

Grease Gun - a tool used to inject grease into grease fittings.

Ground - any metal part of the car. One battery terminal (normally the NEG) is connected to the metal frame to allow the electrical power to make a complete circuit.

H

Head Gasket - the seal between the engine block and cylinder head. A "blown" head gasket will cause low compression and loss of oil or coolant.

Horsepower or **HP** - measurement of the power produced by the engine. See torque.

Hose Clamps - the metal bands which hold the rubber hoses in place and prevent leaks.

Hydraulic - using fluid pressure to transmit a force. See Bleeding.

Hydroplaning - a loss of traction when the car is driven very fast on wet roads.

I

Idle - the minimum operating speed of the engine.

Ignition - producing a spark to ignite the fuel-air mixture inside the engine.

Insert - the rubber part of the windshield wiper blade.

J

Jack - a tool used to lift the car when changing a flat tire.

Jack Stand - a special tool designed to support the weight of the car.

Jumper Cables - the large wires with clamps at both ends used to connect a two batteries during a jump-start.

Jump-Start - connecting two batteries together to start a car with a "dead" battery.

K

Key Switch - operates the starter motor and the accessories.

Knock - the sound made by the engine when the fuel-air mixture is not burning properly. See octane.

KPH or **Kilometers Per Hour** - a measure of the speed of the car. See Speedometer, MPH, and RPM.

L

Leaf Springs - Long flat bars of metal fastened together to absorb bumps. Most commonly used on rear wheels of larger cars/trucks.

Lean - a mixture containing more air (less fuel).

Linkage - any system of cables, levers, springs, and brackets. See fuel pedal.

Lubrication - reducing the friction between moving parts in order to extend the life and performance of the car.

Lug Nuts - the bolts holding the wheel onto the axle.

Lug Wrench or **Tire Tool** - the tool used to remove lug nuts.

M

Manifold - a set of pipes used to move gases from on place to another. For example: intake manifold or exhaust manifold.

Master Cylinder - see primary cylinder.

Motor Mounts - a special large bushing holding the engine or transmission to the frame of the car.

MPG or **Miles Per Gallon** - the number of miles a car can drive on 1 gallon of fuel.

MPH or **Miles Per Hour** - measurement of the speed of the car. See also KPH, RPM.

Muffler - part of the exhaust system used to reduce noise.

Multi-Grade Oil - oil with special additives to control the thickness (or weight) at various temperatures. For example: 10W40 or 5W30 oil.

N

Negative Ground - when the NEGative battery terminal is connected to the metal frame or engine.

NEGative - one of the terminals on the battery (-).

O

Octane - a measurement of the "anti-knock" ability of fuels. The higher octane fuel is more resistant to knocking.

Odometer - measure distance the car has driven.

OEM - Original Equipment of the Manufacturer or dealership parts.

Oil Filter - removes dirt and impurities from the engine oil.

Oil Pressure Indicators - the warning light or pressure gauge.

Oil Pan - the bottom part of the engine where oil is held.

Off Road - driving on wet, bumpy, or soft roads.

Overdrive - an extra gear in the transmission to allow the engine to turn slower at highway speeds for additional fuel economy.

Oxygen Sensor - part of the emission controls that measurers the exhaust gases to determine if the fuel-air mixture is too lean or rich.

P

Parking Brake - brake system used to hold the car when parked.

PCV or **Positive Crankcase Ventilation** - part of the emission controls used to reduce harmful emission from the engine.

Play - the small distance the steering wheel can be moved without causing the front tires to move, or a pedal can moved without causing the system to operate.

Points - part of the standard ignition system which needs to be replaced often. See electronic ignition.

POSitive - one of the terminals on the battery (+).

Power Brakes - using vacuum (suction) from the engine to reduce the amount of force needed to operate the brake pedal.

Power Steering - using a small hydraulic pump to reduce the force needed to turn the steering wheel.

Power-train - parts of the car that transmit the power from the engine to the wheels.

Pressure Cap - see radiator cap.

Primary Cylinder - the part of the hydraulic system where the force (from the foot pedal) is applied. See also secondary cylinder.

PSI or **Pounds per Square Inch** - a measure of pressure, such as the air in the tires or oil pressure.

Q

Quick Charge - charging a car battery in a short time, which can damage the battery. See trickle charge.

R

Rack & Pinion - a type of steering system.

Radial Tire - a tire which can improve handling ability and fuel economy of the car.

Radiator - used to transfer heat from the fluid to the air. Sometimes called a cooler.

Radiator Cap - is the part on the top of the radiator which regulates the pressure inside the radiator.

Radiator Fan - is used to blow air through the radiator.

Rebuilt - a used part which has been repaired and tested.

Remanufactured - a used part which has been completely disassembled, cleaned, repaired, and tested to "like-new" condition.

Redline - the maximum speed of the engine.

Rotor - the part under the distributor cap which turns, or the flat metal part of the disc brake.

RPMs or **Rotations Per Minutes** - is the speed which the parts inside the engine are turning. See MPH, KPH.

S

Secondary Cylinder - responds to the force applied at the primary cylinder. See primary cylinder and hydraulic.

Self Adjusters - the device on rear brakes used to automatically adjust the brake pads.

Sending Unit - the part which "sends" information to the dashboard gauge/light or computer.

Shock Absorber - a part of the suspension used to absorb vibrations and reduce excessive bouncing of the springs.

Shop Manual - the book containing complete instruction about all repairs and maintenance for a car.

Short Circuit - an alternate path (or circuit) in the electrical system which can damage the wires and cause an electrical fire.

Spark Advance - adjusting the distributor (timing) while the engine is running to allow smooth engine operation at all speeds.

Spark Plug - the part of a gasoline engine that produces the spark needed to ignite the fuel-air mixture inside the engine.

Speedometer - the instrument used to measure the speed of the car in MPH or KPH. See tachometer.

Standard Ignition System - uses the points and condenser. See electronic ignition.

Starter - a powerful electric motor needed to turn the parts inside the engine until the fuel-air starts to burn.

Steering System - the parts of the car that allow the steering wheel to control the position of the front wheels.

Strut - a special suspension system where the shock absorber is located inside the coil spring.

Supercharger - is turned by an engine belt and forces air into the engine to produce more power, but decreases fuel economy. See turbocharger.

Suspension System - the parts of the car that support the weight of the car and provide a smooth ride.

Synthetic Oil - oil made from ultra refined petroleum or non-petroleum products.

T

Tachometer - measures the engine speed or how fast parts inside the engine are turning in RPMs. See Speedometer.

TDC or **Top Dead Center** - position used to adjust the engine timing.

Thermostat - is used to regulate the engine temperature.

Tie Rod - part of the steering system. Ball joints are located on the end of the tie rod.

Timing - adjustments made to the ignition system to allow the sparkplugs to operate at the proper time.

Timing Belt - the belt (or chain) inside the engine used to control the engine valves. See valves.

Timing Light - tool used to check or adjust the engine timing.

Tire Valve - where air is added to the tire and the air pressure is checked.

Tire - the rubber part of the wheel.

Toe-In or **Toe-Out** - adjustment of the wheel alignment.

Torque - a measure of the twisting force. See horsepower.

Torque Converter - part of the automatic transmission which acts like a clutch. See clutch.

Torque Wrench - a tool used to precisely tighten a part.

Traction - the ability of the wheels to grip the road surface and avoid skidding or sliding.

Trans-axle - a combination transmission and differential (or axle) used on many front wheel drive cars.

Tread Wear Indicator or **Wear-Bars** - the rubber section molded into the tire to indicates the minimum safe tread.

Trickle Charge - charging the battery slowly to avoid damage to the battery.

Tune-up - adjustments to the engine so that it will start easily, run smoothly, and have normal fuel economy (MPG).

Turbocharger - is turned by exhaust gases leaving the engine and increases the fuel economy and performance of the engine. See supercharger.

Turn - spinning the brake drum or rotor to remove small scratches and produce a very smooth surface.

U

Undercoat - a protective coating applied underneath the car to help prevent rust.

Universal Joint - the flexible connections on the ends of the drive shaft. Also called a CV Joint or Constant Velocity Joint.

V

Vacuum - suction caused by the movement of parts inside the engine.

Vacuum Advance- adjusting the timing of the engine with vacuum from the engine. See also centrifugal advance.

Vacuum Gauge - the instrument used to measure the amount of suction produced by the engine.

Valves - parts inside the engine which allow the fuel-air mixture to enter and the exhaust gases to exit. See timing chain.

Vapor Lock - when the fuel lines are very hot and small bubbles form inside the fuel pump. This can cause the engine to stop.

Viscosity - a measure of the thickness of oil. Higher viscosity means a thicker oil.

Voltage Regulator - controls the electricity produced by the alternator.

W

Warning Light - a small light on the dashboard which indicates an important condition.

Water Pump - circulates the radiator fluid between the engine and radiator.

Water Separator - a special filter on a diesel engine used to remove water from the fuel supply.

Wear-Bars - see tread wear indicators.

Wheel - the rubber tire and metal rim assembly.

Wheel Alignment - the exact position of the tires needed for proper handling, even tread wear and good fuel economy.

Wheel Cylinder - see secondary cylinder.

Wiring Diagram - a drawing of all the wires and electrical devices found in the shop manual.

Wiring Harness - the collection of wires used to transmit electrical power.

INDEX

Other CoNation Publications

The Green Machine

277 pages $12.95

Do you drive a GREEN MACHINE? Discover how to keep your car running safely, economically, and reduce pollution. If you want a long and happy relationship with your car, while at the same time be environmentally friendly, this book can help. You can reduce the cost-per-mile with easy maintenance tips, checklists, and helpful hints for dealing effectively with a mechanic.

For FREE information about all these helpful car care items, send your name and address to CoNation Today.

Car Care Logbook

64 pages $4.95

When did you last change the oil? Last week....last month.... or last year? Don't know? If so, then you need the **Car Care Logbook**. Good written records help keep your car in top shape and increase the resale value. This book contains helpful tips to help you keep your car running great. Order a copy for your car today.

Listen to these audio tapes while driving and you will discover how to drive with confidence and keep your car running great.

Talking About Cars

Audio Tape - 30 minutes $4.95

Listen and learn about your car. Discover how to keep your car in safe and reliable condition with the answers to the most common car care questions. Jim Gaston, host of the radio show **CAR KEYS**, will help you keep your car running great.

Trouble Shooting Tips

Audio Tape - 30 minutes $4.95

Discover easy ways to locate and solve many common car problems. It is easy if you know what to do (or not to do). Even if you cannot solve the problem yourself, knowing more about your car can help you communicate effectively with the mechanic.

Other Audio Tapes

Send your name and address to CoNation and request current information about other audio tapes.

Look for these computer programs on local or national BBS or order directly from CoNation.

Car Care Program

Computer Program (PC) $8.95

This computer shareware program provides useful information about keeping your car running great. Browse through the pop up screens or print out information for later reference.

Tune-Up Program

Tune-Up (PC) $3.00

This computer shareware program describes a typical tune-up and the 5 keys to getting a good tune-up. Find out why the low cost tune-ups are not such a good bargain or end up costing much more than you expected. Don't waste your time or money on expensive tests, which are not needed, and overlook the easy and inexpensive parts which can keep your car running great.

If you are not satisfied, for any reason, return the item along with the sales receipt to the place of purchase for a complete refund.

Testimonials

What experts are saying about

When There's No Mechanic

by Jim Gaston

" Helpful information and trouble shooting tips."
- The Bookwatch

". . . everyday language and well documented."
- George Hensel, editor
Driving School Association of America

" This books describes how to keep your car running, what service it needs, or does not need. Keep a copy in the glove compartment."
- News Press
St Joseph, MO

" When There's No Mechanic contains specific information in well organized chapters. It is a very helpful and easy to follow guide."
- Patrician Productions, NY

" As host of the weekly radio program **CAR KEYS**, Jim Gaston's help with peoples automotive problems is much appreciated."
- Jim Sackett
WDNC Radio

Order Form

Name:_____

Address:_____

_____ZIP_____

BOOKS
   _ When There's No Mechanic $12.95
   _ The Green Machine $12.95
   _ Car Care Logbook $ 4.95

AUDIO TAPES
   _ Talking About Cars $ 4.95
   _ Trouble Shooting Tips $ 4.95

COMPUTER PROGRAMS (PC)
   _ Car Care Program $ 8.95
   _ Tune-Up Program $ 3.00

TOTAL _____

Full Refund If Not Completely Satisfied

(NC Residents add 6% Sales Tax)
FREE Shipping to USA / Canada
Faster AIR MAIL shipping, Add $2 per Item

Send A Check or Money Order To:

CoNation Publications
703-W Ninth Street
Durham NC 27705

Or Call 1-800-826-6600

Classic MotorBooks   Orders Only Please